just to tell the truth

Leon Ramsey

iUniverse, Inc.
New York   Bloomington

iUniverse books may be ordered through booksellers or by contacting:

iUniverse
1663 Liberty Drive
Bloomington, IN 47403
www.iuniverse.com
1-800-Authors (1-800-288-4677)

ISBN: 978-1-4401-2546-1 (sc)
ISBN: 978-1-4401-2545-4 (ebook)

Printed in the United States of America

iUniverse rev. date: 03/19/2009

INTRODUCTION

I have A few Interesting Bits of life. Thanks To The Help of Modern Doctors And Being told No Idea Why i am Still Alive And Kicking And More Shocking Is how This has Happen ?And What is Going on To make Sure No one will know about this ?And for All The people who Treated me like i had No Brain and cant Speak English !This is to Show the Truth. Thanks to all The Great Doctors Who Helped me More Than the Rest And One Real Doctor Who i was Told to do and i did Call Him at Home Dr Charles Hillenbrand .When I thought the end was near due to the Pain of so many Broken Bones like Hip, upper ribs, Arms, Fingers,As well as Smashed Skull and after a Quick i call tune up I Got Back on the Track to life and smiled kept on Going and a lot more Thanks To All Of You Lee

This is a Start to a story But I called much more like eventful,Because Waking up in a Hospital Have no idea how i got there?But Worse off is to look around and see and feel how bad your own body is and what is left ?But more of a shock is feeling something is wrong?I cant Hear a thing and my vision like real Strange Double two of everything ?All i can do is tell my self Keep your lid on you are okay in a hospital but which one ?Where am I,I can see nurses walking up to me checking bandages taking pulse,Lee how are you the nurse is asking me and writhing it down as well!I pick up my right arm okay !I feel pain from all the staples in my hip and leg very sharp i want to yell But the next words from the nurse like reading the same brain ,I will get you Something for the pain !As i am trying to look around and see out the window but i cant even pick my self enough to much pain !But there is a small thing from the past next to this event ?I am missing half my leg due to a motorcycle accident like hit and run .That is nothing next to this one ?All the pain was in my smashed up leg hit by a 1969 Delta 88 car doing about 50 to 55MPH Six months in the hospital and 17 operations later Gangrene set in off with leg as well as the pain was gone 3 months later back to work !So many people asking where have i been on Vacation ?I tell yea lost my leg in a bike accident people say sure you look fine ,I pull up my pants leg and show them the fiberglass leg So many jaws hit the floor and i walk away laughing .But now I sit in a hospital much more worse off ?I have No idea what happen where or when ?Do I scream or start yelling what the hell is going on ?Just as i am about to push the panic button a nurse gives me a shot for the pain I lay back and try to see is this a Dream ?I have no idea,I am so relaxed pain is floating away Great and a lady comes up to the side of the bed She Starts writing something down on a piece of paper?Lee how are you?Do you know who i am ?I tell her I am okay But who are you ?I am your Wife !What is your name K I push my self back trying to think this out fast Great I have a wife I asked her what happen to me and why am i here She stays back from me and tells me you were run over at work 14 days ago ?I feel like i just was told something But I have no idea When i try to think about this it is blank?And she stays back All i can think is I must really be messed up not any type of feelings no kiss or touching She starts asking me Questions do i have any idea what Happen did you see anything ?NO I have No Idea at all ?You worry

1

about it later,Get better get out of here. You have Three Sons do you remember any of them No again She tells me she will let me go to sleep and see you later and leaves. Now i know the old saying out to lunch I have no idea about a thing at all And a few days go by other people from work come to see me again do you have any idea what happen and No again !So as i learn to talk again add math and try to get me going But no leg to walk with I have asked doctors they tell no it will take time due to your balance problem ?And i have no thoughts on this balance at all So now i sit up in bed try to watch TV I feel like any day and i go home just as i feel okay a person from work manager comes to see me And First words out of his mouth again Do you have any idea what happen ?No But what he says next starts a Fireball!Lee Glad to hear that all of us at work building came up with a answer you walked into a incoming tractor it is your fault !I asked him to leave my room I am getting tried so he leaves Thank God !I lay back trying to think about this and no answer ! Now the picture of where I work is about to be told After having some of this starting to take place. After being so afraid of saying where i work and what i do for a living I work for a large airline have been in a couple of cities where i started New Yorker at 18yrs old and very happy Because in 1974 I started at 4.10 hr working midnights shift I went home to Brooklyn NY Holding on to my stomach it was so sore from laughing and having a great time at work !Felt very much like a person and it seems after going to San Francisco, Chicago it has very much gone away. Laughing or having a good day at work And being at one of the large airlines you can see the rotten place to work just look for people outside who forget how to smile of laugh I was a person who wants to work very much and did the best to make sure i was so happy getting awards at work and the day off with pay All i did was look to see what else i could do to make it better I worked the mail area by my self to start with a very good person with a brain said Lee here is the book and paper work read it and run the area the way you want any problems call me at the office I will come and see you I thought it was a joke but it is not !Went home read what i could about some strange things and operations and rules .Next day in a working area by my self trying to make it work as about 15 or 16 co workers came to me and said What do you want us to do ?Now i know what thrown to the fire means And i did it After 8hrsof this the person who gave this

to me came up to me at the end of the day and said You did Great I did
not get one call about what you did or did not do!Great Start when you
are 6foot 4in 230lbs and no problems who wants to start any thing .
Being from Brooklyn helps So as i did work area get to know the people
who want to work with me .And start the fun and again I break all
kinds of records like amount of mail through area And the amount left
over night so the company would not be fined But as largest amount of
mail moved out of city What really helped was told no sick calls. I made
sure no one bothered us at work area and tried to make so many workers
smile at work helped and laugh and have Good days at work it went on
for a long time And as three yrs go by with records broken and people
wanting to come to my working area I was very proud of it Again happy
to go to work laugh and have a good time at work But it seems to start
when you do supervisors reports and paper work I did not even get
thanks or anything when you have a good day at work you hated Well
it looks like it is time to do something else and where?So off to a
different place and do nothing !I was so mad of this mind games taken
place by a supervisor i decided to go to area and do nothing how long
would it last I get a list of things to do and in 4hrs i am done So i go
around asking other people do they need any help and try to help other
workers only to be told get out of here or leave me alone take a walk !So
as i am 35yrs old and doing nothing at work i keep my chin up and try
even more thing at work to do So off to the different work area i go post
office and i like it better and people i work with from the past are now
at post office as well and working together and doing something feels a
lot better so i will stay here i hope because i am getting calls from
supervisors to come and help them in my old work place and asking
questions how to run the place I tell them papers in desk draw start
reading to learn how to run the place and hang up the phone !And now
i can see why so many crabby people at work I try to tell jokes or even
smile only to get some upsetting remarks !I try not to think about this
and start doing things at home much better off i have one son who is
4yrs old and Twin boys that are 2yrs old and i really like it i may be bald
soon what the hell. I have a wife who says she cant handle twins wants
to give them up for adoption ?I tell her no I will work nights and be
home all day with the sons and did it ,I would meet her after work put
sons in her jeep sleeping or take my Ford Van and go to work as she

goes home puts sons in bed sleeping and what she wants ?What is the question can she handle this and what could she be doing as she is home alone ? Well you are a happy father working your wife is home You have a nice Home in a very nice Neighbor hood and now really understand you have built a family that you never saw in past or grew from And do you stop and Think is it okay or is there something out of place ?no take it easy Grow up don't get nervous you are fine ?So on my lunch time while most foregoing out to lunch at 2:00am i am 20min to home I take off on my way do not see one person car truck cat dog etc. It looks like the side walks are rolled up As i pull into driveway very quiet walk threw the house see that all is sleeping sons are fine all covered up I walk to check on wife i walk over cover her up as well not a word .I head back to work very slowly and all is quiet and much better inside all is fine !or is it These are some things going through the mind as i am in the hospital busted up pretty bad .Good thinking of past to keep going Now all i can think is get better and get out of this place to be home with family .I keep telling my self you will be okay God kept you alive for something Keep going this is what i have told my self inside I have a Good reason to make it Don t give up over and over dont give up AS i get better with the help As many doctors com ming to see me asking questions about do i know how or what happen ?And it is like a robot answering no i have no idea at all One doctor says in time you will get the answer to keep this going !And i do with little things like I am talking and the words are not all connected together ?I try to read newspaper with one eye covered up to try stop this double vision it works I am reading and i don't feel right ?Have one eye covered up and all of sudden the lights go out in my room I get pissed i start yelling very loud turn the lights on AS i am holding the paper one nurse tells me Lee the lights are on I tell her i cant see a thing are you sure about that now i can feel lots hands touching telling me to lay down ?We will call your doctor ASAP I can feel my heart going pounding away I tell my self take easy Dr. R will give you the answer as he comes and sees you relax you are okay Now i am upset I can hear the doctors voice telling me Lee you will be in surgery in the morning your eyes have collapsed don't worry we will fix it in the morning   So I lay in bed wondering the next part of this master picture story!Will i see again Will i not make it threw the operation ?And the most unreal part is how did this happen to me how did i get so mashed up at work ?So much of this What happen to me after all This time in hospital still no answers to this !Now all i have to do is get threw this operation again !So at 0700 nurses came to tell me I am being taken to surge to work on my eyes . Great I can see after this i am telling my self Don't worry only to get better and see again. I can hear something but not sure A voice calling me Lee, Lee, it is your wife calling I cant see but someone grabs my arm are you okay?Glad i caught you before they get you into the room Give me a kiss on the head walks away Good luck see you when wake up So as i go into the operation room I hear a nurse asking me questions can i see yet I tell her No not yet. The doctor will put a line or tube in the back of your head to get the pressure off your brain If any fluid is in there it will drain in to your stomach,Don t worry you will be okay I can feel IVs put into my arm I feel like it is going away ,Next thing i know i am waking up in recovery room About to give back what ever is in my guts. I can see but real fuzzy and i know i did not drink a beer I grab my eye lids sure is nice to see my own fingers !Tape in on my eye brows I pull it off i tell a nurse as she comes to see me I tell her i am going to get sick real soon as she hands me a bowl like thing i fill it up with nasty tasting stuff. And a FEW SECONDS LATER I feel much better my gut claim down all i can think is i am going to make it I can see a little better and still talk English I will be okay nurse after taking my pulse says ready to go back to your room ?I tell yes and off i go a few second later Great i am being pushed back to my room Now i can see where i am going now Not Bad !The aid pushing my bed down the hall way asks me what happen to me how did i get hurt so bad all over I could tell her I was run over at work She said you look okay keep going so you can get out of this place I told her i am trying ! And back in my room at last all i feel like doing is sleep after being forced to sleep due to medications I was hoping to see my wife and sons that sure would get better faster !But no such luck .I really don't like the out come of this surly,I have to much bandages around my head   but I am to stay in bed and lay flat for two weeks and cant get up ?Now i see why i am strapped down to the bed !This ought to be fun going to the bathroom. I don't think i can hold it in for two weeks And just as i get relaxed a nurse pops in With Lee I have to talk to you about the surly you just had I told her fill me in You have to stay flat till your Head gets back to

Normal because the doctor messes with the fluid in your Head and around the Brain !It is low on fluid till it gets better you will have a real balance problem. So just relax most people sleep a lot to make it easy and more time to get the fluid built up I said okay i will do what i can ,she tells me nurses will come in and bath you fix up your bed and if the pain starts getting bad push the buzzer we will keep you relaxed I tell her Thanks for the help and have you heard from my wife?She said yea she called when you were still in surly,We told her you are okay that was it .I said thanks for telling me i will take a nap now see ya later !I lay back the best i can all covered up and try to sleep wondering what is going on at home ?How are the Sons doing and hears well and as i fade away and go to sleep wondering How did i get so mashed up ?Who did this to me No way did i walk into a incoming tractor Something is missing ?Like why wont any one from work come and see me ?I know i am not a Bad Guy !Something is really strangeness was hit years ago on my sporty coming home from work plenty of people came to see me in hospital 6 months no problem Even when my leg was amputated some one came to see me .But what is going on this time ?I am suppose to be sleeping but my black and blue Brain wont let me sleep I can remember laughing when any one came to see me and i was making so much noise laughing and make the best out of me really smashed up leg !That is how i know God is watching me i was coming home from work at about 930pm in a nice July night going through a inner section at two big roads And here comes a 1969 Delta 88 moving 50 to 55mph all i saw next to me was two head lights to make sure it does not go over me i opened up the throttle and i was lucky he spun me around as i left the inter section flying threw the air landed on the road. I tried to get up but left leg was like not working ?I look down to see the femur sticking up through my jeans Blood was like a hose coming out even further down my leg both bones threw my leather boots and they were hi sided boots !I tell my self real loud Damn it inside i lay back down and a person from work put his black van side ways across the road so i don't get hit again. Comes over Lee hang in there i tell this person F thanks Any one call a Ambulance yea it is on the way about two blocks away and that is how far the hospital is two blocks !paramedics tried to put some mask on my face i yelled get the f away from me ! and passed out And put me in the ambulance and a few seconds later a officer comes over to me tell me they caught the kid driving the Sherman tank delta 88 And he will come and see me in the Hospital .when you are okay I tell him thanks see later and off i go to the hospital !That was July 1981 Sure is very real at 27yrs old Change in your life is about to happen. All i can do is tell my self make it, make it,make it you will make it no matter what !As i can hear the doors of the ambulance open up and nurses yelling on what to do as each does her part to help me through this ,I see a nurse pass out and hit the floor .Now i am wondering man you must be really busted up !I can see IVs are being put in my arms and here is a doctor telling me his name is Ralph as my clothes are now all gone and blood is on it all .hi Lee he tells me some words it sounds like God will step in any second ?If we can save your leg we will But if not we will do the best we can ,Lay back we will put you out for a few days till the bleeding stops and you are okay !I tell him good luck thanks for your help and out i go !So as i am under getting the body put back together again I came to three days later And i can not understand if i am dreaming or Dead and gone looking around to see life to people my eye sight is so bad i see this long white thing what is it bloody ?As i look and see the end of this goes to my body I am happy as hell inside it is my leg still there All i can think is thanks to God my leg is still mine i will be okay but it is only the start to Six months in the hospital and seventeen surges and i tell my self you made it no problems and in that time a few people came to see me in the hospital I really believe that is why i made it after all the trauma st was due to friends coming to see me really helps And i lost the leg a year later due to gangrene setting in Went back to work 4 months later after loosing leg Walking so good people asking me where have i been on vacation !

But if not we will do the best we can ,Lay back we will put you out for a few days till the bleeding stops and you are okay !I tell him good luck thanks for your help and out i go !So as i am under getting the body put back together again I came to three days later And i can not understand if i am dreaming or Dead and gone looking around to see life to people my eye sight is so bad i see this long white thing what is it bloody ?As i look and see the end of this goes to my body I am happy as hell inside it is my leg still there All i can think is thanks to God my leg is still mine i will be okay but it is only the start to Six months in the hospital and seventeen surges and i tell my self you made it no problems and in that time a few people came to see me in the hospital I really believe that is why i made it after all the trauma st cuff due to friends coming to see me really helps And i lost the leg a year later due to gangrene setting in Went back to work 6months later after loosing leg Walking so good people asking me where have i been on vacation ! You look Great glad to see you back to work!And now i am wondering why no one will come and see me ?And i am suppose to be Married and i thought your partner is to be with you and take care of you no matter what?And i am just get better!and don't think about it not yet. May be i am just paranoid better off telling myself relax don't think of it .It hurts pretty Good inside,worry about it later. So I must have had a Good nap!Be because a nurse is waking me up taking my pulse asking me am I okay I tell her sure okay,But this sucks,Tells me be right back with a shot hang on And it is like a Genie next thing She is pulling my sheets off me and putting a shot on the side of the cheeks,Bingo shot time back to who knows where i go again No one in the room Damn just sleep again!   So after all of this fun 13 days later Doctor tells me i can get up i ask him how about the leg?Can i try to walk yet,No you are still in the wheel chair but pretty soon we will try ,you have to get a little bit better and stronger ,you keep doing what you are ,I will let you know!So believe it or not but 5 months pulls up ,I have had enough of this stuff,Time to walk today. I feel pretty good still cant hear much it looks like i put some weight on. I think i can do it,Well here it is 0700am in the morning I am tired of taking bird baths ,Let the nurse wash some one else look around no one coming or going I get to edge of the bed put leg over the side feels Great I sit there for about 30 minutes feeling better more and more. I reach over grab a towel and hop to the shower Happy as Hell. Hanging on to any thing possible just to make sure i don't fall over. I turn on the water Man nice and warm ,Grab the soap just as i was about to start washing I can hear nurses yell my name on the p/a system My last name louder and louder Never mind i am taking a nice shower 5 months All i can think is they will see me later where i am going .Water feels great just as i wash my hair ,The door opens up i could hear the nurse say we will call your Doctor on this event I said i am done now I will be glad to get some clothes on ! And now i feel pretty good getting better this time in the hospital I am at least trying to get on with life as hard or not! I hope i get home soon that would be a great way to get better stay home help wife and sons. It sure would be nice I have been here 5 months I guess I will make it to much of no information on this if i am home maybe I can color the picture to what has taken place the large question to who what, where,and when is getting Bigger and Bigger after all this time still cant remember a thing ?I am so tied up trying to get better and all the Doctors nurses,Not much time to do much else but get better .It sure is strange not to have any help on this from work No one has called me or come to see me now I know what it is like when you have bad breath or a Diseases all stay away But why Well now i get told by nurse tomorrow i will have a Cat Scan to the Head and not to eat anything after 900pm This is to see if i am getting good enough to go home with out any problems .I tell the nurse great .home at last,She says you have been here long enough just for something to do I go threw the cabinet get rid of what is not needed .Get all my clothes put in bags to carry our of here. Call wife to come and get me at last to come home!But as i tell her I may come home she says she will call me later,she is calling work to see if see can get the day off from work,She will let me know later ,After that call,I was hoping to hear something Different maybe I have been in this place to long?I thought 5 months was enough sleeping by self,She said she had trouble with sons sleeping with her due to Dad not being there!Sons would not stay in there beds I asked her don't you want to hang on to me instead of sons?She said she will see when i get home?Now i am puzzled inside,like you hear so many sayings Time will tell or you will know when you see them,Now i am in one of those sayings and inside something is very much Wrong and it looks like i have to put it together my self. But something is missioning is getting late around 1130pm the hospital floor is very quiet I think this is the best time No Doctors sticking someone and on one is yelling look out side see all the lights on all the building so many lights to see and in the morning all gone. I will hear from the doctors some great answers go home or stay .Time to get some sleep and be ready for a great day !! Made it threw again,Get cleaned up ready for the Doctor have some Breakfast get ready. Like your inner body is getting you ready plenty of energy to go .All my things are in hospital plastic bags to go .One small suit case like things with strap to carry out of here. Just as i sit down on side of the bed. Doctor walks in looks me over asks me how i am Doing inside and the most asked question so far how is the pain doing ?I tell him i am getting used to it .He says Good looks like you should go home to your family and get going. I tell him Thanks for all the things to do and teach me. Put out my hand we both shake hands he says good luck any more problems or you don't feel okay call my office and they will get in touch with me okay. And out the door he goes,Now if i could just slow down my heart beat just a little am so Happy time to get home I call home ask wife to come and get me,time to go home. But what comes out of her mouth next. I am twisted inside,I will call work and see if i can get time off to come and get you I will call you right back!I tell her okay I will sit and wait for your call as she hangs up i am really Wondering what the hell is taken place?Heart racing blood pressure hitting almost the roof of the Hospital. Time to walk down the hall to claim down and cant believe i am thing who else to call just in case to get me home and come up with a person brother in law almost back to my room i sit down phone rings she says she has to work but she called brother in law he will get me home instead. She says see will see me later hangs up the phone talk about upset and i am not even out of Hospital yet?About 35 minutes later he walks in my room says Hi grabs my bags of stuff and out the door we go as i walk past the nurses station so many nurses out loud saying Good Luck,And Bye-Bye I did it,As we get to his van not very much feel like talking but it seems very fast I am home all Three Sons running up to the van yelling Dad Dad Sons grabbing my legs hanging on .As i walk into the house she is not home ?And baby sitter watching the sons He caries my things in the house and is gone !I try telling him Thanks and backs out of the drive way I walk around the house and had no idea about my Balance problem taking place due to the carpet thickness. And i don't drink but you would think i had to many Beers or something and three sons follow me around from behind asking am i okay?I tell them i have to learn how to walk again they start laughing. Dad we will help you okay,I tell them Thanks for the help It is something for a 5yr old son to offer to help you and his twin brother follow to and are 3yrs old all sticking together. That last for a long time to come they will see after walking around i tell sons and baby sitter I will lay down and take a Knapp all take off running out the door to the front yard yelling My Dad is home !I lay down and in a matter of seconds ,I am out sleeping !And 2hrs later wake up from sons pushing me back and forth on the bed .Dad wake up come on we want to be with you !And i sit up a few seconds and try to get up but stop a few seconds and get my balance caught up with me and off i go I walk to back yard and see sons on the swings playing around,Glad i made it home inside feel pretty good and i have noticed the pain in hips and side of head are not to bad !!   Being like this both medically and mentally is very hard to live with and i guess after my bumpy ride down the road .I better let some of this out it is a lot to carry by your self I thought i had a partner to share life with and build a nice family and put the past venture at the end. But i wonder It is very simple i had a Mother and Father who i think like to fight each other and live that way. My Father was a Ground pounder Marine in 1952 or 53 some where around there And my Mother was a polish ladies Daughter and had Three sisters and one brother in Brooklyn NY. But some where got married had Four Kids Two Girls and two Boys and did not know what to do or not do !Because I can Remember moving so many times to parts of Brooklyn, Jersey,and upstate NY way up there like about 30 minutes to Canada from the Farm land And all along fights between my Mother and Father,She had so many Broken Bones and did nothing about it Till i was about 11yrs old packed her bags took two younger kids One Sister and one Brother .So my self and sister lived with Father this happen in 1962 So i lived with father and sister for years and in about 1965 I came home from school ready to go fishing Father said i have to go see my mother in the City Brooklyn NY with my Sister He said he was hit with court paper and we have to go !Now i Don t know what to do or what the picture is next to do ?So late at night we were taken to Watertown NY and put on a Bus to Brooklyn NY Now i am about 12yrs old and have to go to someplace i have no idea about all i can do is think where is this place and where is my fishing going to be And i have to give up my best Friend Belgium Shepard bike and my fishing!We slept and woke 4 or 5 times and switching buses!I think it took two days to get there. As well pull into Port Authority and see so many people as we go threw the doors into the lobby a lady Grabs my sister and says i am your Mother ! Like Gee Great like am suppose to be Happy!We get into a 64 Chevy station wagon see my other sister and brother .We all said Hi and I sat like in the corner looking around. Big Apple as we go to Brooklyn. We get to this large apartment building and my Grand Mother grabs me with a big Hug and in polish words glad to see ya!Next day into court building in down town Brooklyn I see my Father I walk over to him he grabs me and says ,No matter what happens you may have to grow up fast ,But you make it Don't give up !As we go in to this huge Court room I was called by the judge and asked who do i want to live with ?I said my Father Thanks we will see per Judges answer a few seconds as we all stand up And the judges starts Reading this paper saying our names and we are to live in Brooklyn NY with Mother !I Stood up and tried to say No i am living with my Father ,Judge said Sorry you go with your Mother ,I said i was running away to upstate NY to get home ,Judge talked out loud ,WE will put your Father in jail till i am found and with Mother !My Father said you go with your Mother I will see what i can do about this!I never said another word for days. Here i am going on 14yrs old in New York have no idea what to do or where to go fishing or do anything that i liked to do. I liked so much to ride horses run threw the woods watching Deer walking around All Gone Never saw my father again till i was 18yrs old Now i am 6'4" 200lbs and mad as hell hate everything and everyone Because I go to some place and give up all the things i really like to be around I am a outside person .   There are so many things like this when i was young. Even when i had some really nice Girl Friends some went on for years. Some would say you are not going out with who ever .you should break it up before it gets to close Well i was so happy when i was out of school found a job!All i did was work and what ever shift they wanted I did not care .That was so strange with the job at the airlines When ever they needed over time i took it most Overtime the time once i took still remember the most i was called at home to come to work on my day off to work 8 hrs. and this was on the Fourth of July Once there and did 8hrs.over Time. And i was asked to work 8 hrs more So now 16hrs. overtime on a Holiday on my day off 32hrs.pay in one day!Man when i get home and slept 12hrs no problem. All i could do was work save money up and get out of New York asap!With the old saying Go West Young Man !I really liked Denver.Co.I went there and went north to the mountains just looking around so many times .I was so relaxed being there thought it would be a nice to live and do all the Fishing and some hunting camping way out in the woods. That was my dream while being in the Concrete capital New York and when i had a layoff in the Big apple I could stay home or take transfer to San Francisco Ca. Well time to go West .I worked at San Francisco for 11 months and been in two earth quakes, Time to move on I kept going to the beaches ofter work just sitting watching the shore change looking at the water was okay Drove to the mountains many times but it is not enough. Denver was better .I went to personal for a transfer information was told only opening was Chicago ?I have never been there ,I went for job interview to work out side and i Got it. Have to be there in Seven Days. I went home packed my stuff had most of it in my 1978 Chevy Mona 2+2 and off i went to Chicago had a map on the front seat as my car was full of stuff like food pops in a little cooler with ice and i am Gone. I took my time going because i would to be in one piece. The window were so packed you could not see out the back window .I knew where the tools were just in case and 16hrs.later i was there Getting off I 80heading north to I55 looking for planes as i went north as i drove threw Chicago seeing all the tall buildings it looked like NY i kept going this was Monday afternoon as i get to the side of o hare airport I was glad to see it was looking where to go and looking for a place to live found some hotels to stay for tonight as i was to tired to do much more Driving! And the next day i was up driving around a New Town looking for a place to live after eating breakfast at 0800am looking at some news papers try to understand it seeing apartments and how much for rent i liked the north west villages .Asked the cashier as i was leaving for directions how to get to Rolling Meadows gave me some kind of idea so i go for it !Well as i have been driving for about 31/2 hrs and found nothing ?I have no idea where Rolling Meadows is I pull into a stores parking lot get out to get the blood back into my legs standing felt great I am really uptight. I have to start tomorrow and try again and at 0600am I have not found a place yet But i have to be at the airport for new identification and all of that stuff look around and see how to get thereafter see how a new place to work looks I find a back road to the airport and a guards shack there I tell them what i am doing they tell me which way to go and i get off and great i did it again new mug shot and i really like what i saw plenty other people doing the same thing!And on company bus to parking lot was nice to see the aircrafts so close on the taxi ways I have a good feeling being there and real happy about it all!Dot know a soul here so what will meet plenty when i start working i will bet on it !My first year here was very interesting we all know about a very large snow storm winter of 78/79 I was one of few workers who made it to work?I thought many times driving to work cant see much, roads were pretty snowed in I just took my time driving in and made it to work. And after 4hrs at work were sent home all the airport was shut down I am in a new place I thought i had to be at work and try it But to see snow so bad and aircraft engines were all most totally covered up with snow and forget about runways it was like they disappeared like a genie stepped in and made a big Flash all gone !But it was part of life And a working young man !What the hell do it. And years go by never saw another storm like that one was And kept working year after year till the summer of 1981 was 27 yrs old and at 930pm coming home from work on a new XLH sportster and about 45MPH Happy as hell Few more blocks to go I stopped put in some Gas for tomorrow and my ears were getting cold put on Helmet put in my $4.00 to top off the Gas Tank....

I start it up leave the gas station drive nice and easy show off my clean ride on the right side of the road getting closer to a intersection which is on a bad angle of the road looks like a pair of lessors half closed I was in the middle of it the section. I just happen to look to my left side and see a pair of headlights coming Fast getting closer. And i don't feel like touching them now So i pulled on the Throttle fast as much as i could thinking he might spin me around instead of going over me ?When a Delta 88 1969 is ab out to go over you You can think fast or else That is what happen I did not think he would touch me But the next thing i know i am flying threw the air looking what the hell is this I see a shopping center and getting closer faster passing up one light pole see people standing watching me !I hit the Ground by The edge of the street and next to the sidewalk .Happy as hell i made it Great I tried to get up but something was wrong and a lot of pain in leg I looked down at my leg and see bones sticking up threw my boots and pants Femur threw the upper part of my pants and blood pouring out all over the place?And lower bones went threw my boot I had on tall boots with bones sticking threw both sides. I tell myself lay down quickly you are not walking anywhere. And try to relax and one person from work was behind me coming home as well from work. He puts his 1978 Dodge Van behind me blocking off the road so not to get hit again laying in the road way A person named FM was great he comes running over to me are you okay?I said i am trying I asked him where is the hospital about two blocks away don't worry ambulance is on the way!and one officer comes over said we got the kid that ran you over I will see you in a few days Take care Good luck and asked for my driving license all i had him was a permit all was about two months old and a new Bike with number one jug snapped off and that is where my leg was As the Ambulance pulls up asks me if i want any gas to breath till we get to the hospital I start yelling No get me to the F in hospital?As they lift me up slid a board under me i yelled put me in and off we go to hospital K telling me he will see me tomorrow in the hospital I tell thanks for the help see ya and when you have a bad feeling about the mess i am in I wonder will i make it or not Like a bad dream a few seconds later we are backing in the hospital ER door open. I made it but the fun is just starting .You know you are in bad shape when you see nurses pass out and hit the floor and hear couple other yelling and leaving by me fast?As i get into the room it was strange my clothes disappear IVs in my arms fast and some Doctor comes over tells me his name Ralph Good Luck next was very strange he tells me if he can save my leg he will But if not I will do the best i can We will keep you out for a few days till the bleeding slows down and i feel the medications starting and out i go   I wake up three days later but I could not see to Good enough my vision was bad at night time could not see to understand what this white thing hanging in front of my bed was,I try to follow it to the end but it seem to be going to towards me?As my eye sight got some what better it looked like it was one of my legs tried to put my hand on it to touch it!But could not reach it It was my leg It was still there Great I will be okay i thought I laded back trying to get my brain to think what happen seemed real slow to get started I know i am i a hospital but what do i do next?And some nurse comes over asks me how i feel i said okay but how am i doing this leg thing,She said they saved it but you are in real serious shape they rebuilt bones and pinned you up pretty good you will be with no for some time to come don't worry,I said okay but it seemed like very strange i was feeling pain coming on and like lots of it!I asked the nurse who was standing there watching me ,why is the pain getting so bad right now?She said you were under for a few days now you are awake and so is the pain you had a lot of busted bones and do you have any idea how much was busted?No she said all your toes ankle were so smashed up and all pinned together Both your lower leg bones fibula fibula were missing long puces of the bone and that is where you bone graft is started but don't worry you Doctor will be in soon and fill you in on this,Here is your first shot for pain you can get it every 4 hours just in case it gets bad,And walks away now i am wondering what is going on i must be worse off then i thought and saw happen to me And as the Doctor came in tell me even more right down to the end of his mess he just tried to fix up and put me together!But asked me if i can call anyone to come and see me I gave him my mother and fathers name and phone number. He said he will call them about this matter and come and see you .I said good luck for getting me back together He said you will be with us for some time I will have some one call your job don't worry get better do as nurses ask to get you better and out of here. Well would believe me if i said i spent six months in the hospital and seventeen operations later on top of that I meet a nurse who would stop a train she was very Beautiful and had a brain from Nashville. Every day she took care of me was so nice to talk with and i would hate to say when i got out of this hospital we liver together !and got married three years later back to being by my self one thing that started it was I am not sure how someone can try to tell you when you can do what ever or when. I came out of shower hit in the face with a wet towel and told get Dressed we are going shopping !Well the towel got returned to the same place on her and said you F____n go and divorce time .So be it !

She goes her way i go mine I go to work now only now it is work and home no more going out to find a partner. All i want to do is go camping get back into going places again. I went back to New York to see friends that still call each other friends from 13 and 14 yrs old still call each other now at 49yrs old we still call each other caressing i have learned from past mother has not seen me for about 17yrs who knows why father saw me once in the hospital but he came to my apartment few times to see me and it went fast like no time it will be to come and see son again!I kept working and trying to be happy bought a lot of clothes and one 4x4 Bronco truck to make sure if i get hit some how i have metal around me to protect my body. I learned after loosing my leg from the knee down is to cover your self. I watched on more thing I did. Now more than ever Now at work out side I watch every step i took so as not to fall and get hurt I checked shoes i wore everything !Make sure my door was locked so many things I learned to do And then as i Get work going again won awards to work and get the day off with pay,Plus a$500.00 bones it was real good inside i tried not to make my self left out due to being Amputee. So what I have had a few jaws hit the floor in mens locker room Changing clothes and pop off leg and changed pants so many co workers eyes fell out .Had even joked have you been stumped lately?And it really helped so many to understand me as well as them seeing me it was okay after all and there is truth to doctors telling me about dreams I still have I still have a leg because my toes will be Archie or i can feel the leg jump up and down at bed time wondering what that was .The best one to get your attention is I have gone to a pool popped off my leg and jumped in leaving leg next to the pool so many people look at you I will swim around get to side put leg on and walk away feeling nice and cooled off .After all of this fun things to life already I wonder if i would try again to have a partner I am tried of this run around by my self It would be nice to be hanging on to a warm lady at bed time. Sleeping by my self really sucks. I have a four legged dog but that don't make it .Getting older means you should share life With a mate partner someone?Thought it should happen but i have not tried because i would not want a nice looking lad pass out when you tell them about your fiberglass leg just in case you have the hots for someone i don't want to hear you are okay but cant handle the leg part you are missing like i am not a man due to being amputee,I have been working a lot just to keep my mind of of this. I have had enough pain and need a break for a while and charge my battery. I will wait and see maybe someone i will meet someday will have a back bone and be strong enough to handle it all !

And instead of worrying I will just keep on working I have some old friends from the past i have been going out to the Range blasting some targets at 200 yd s. And it is Great to just keep my mind on the target and nothing else!I like my own therapy And doing that i feel like the treat nothing different. And now when i feel like it i take a Drive in a old Vet t 78 silver all redone real nice and clean looks like new and just drive I have gone to lake Geneva and back by my self And i am not doing it to find some one !But my self need the way to feel better about mt leg bothering me and a few times i had to pull over pop off the leg ,put it in the back and get home getting cramps sucks. I have tried to get used to the idea .I am a little different on the out side but the same in side my feelings have been run over a few times but what the hell i keep trying an way i live by my self it is hard some times. And i still have the Brain telling me don't give up now You have along way to go i wonder if i was taking shower and standing with one leg and she see it what would happen. Some of these things will just have to see about .when guys from work saw it you could see the look in there eyes. Like what the hell is he doing And I just changed my clothes a little quicker. After a while i stopped changing clothes wore my uniform there and back. It was okay after a while i was on the first bus leaving the terminal an way. Got home a few minutes early i really stop thinking about going threw this mind stuff for a while I was okay i know not getting hurt inside i would be better off. And now on my days off i would just not make plans to do much it i wanted to travel to Denver New York where ever I just went .As you can see as i say so much about being by my self so much i think it is how to keep going is so strong. In the back of the mind you do a lot to make sure you don't get hurt inside or out gives a lot of energy Like you are building a strong new home to make sure it does not go down in the first storm .Still standing looks great no problems is how i feel inside doing lots of walking at work on your feet 8hrs either driving tractors or working around aircraft in side all the movement helps the body get used to the new body part But don't let it fool you .When i first went to work in November about 5 or 6 weeks later i was changing my clothes in the locker room as i took off the leg I got real lite headed all i could see was Red lots of it !all around the special sock was bloody .I tell my self don't panic look and see what it is and how to fix it .It turns out as told in the start of this your body will build up the skin and make it tougher as the skin now has different spots to hold your body weight on and sores will bleed and get tougher. I wait a few seconds get the blood pressure to go down. I hop over to the sink pull up my pant leg and wash off the blood and socks and hop back to locker and get it back together i have clean fresh socks I put on and on the leg goes sore as hell put the bloody ones in the bag to get them home and washed up Talk about my first lesson what a thing to learn it was a crash course. And i kept cool and did fine. I have seen guys at work panic when they cut there finger from sacks of mail go almost running to medical for a bandied!those are the ones i watch out for in case they really get hurt!

As i get my self put back together with no red stuff laying around or on me i am really glad to head for home did my 8hrs.Time to relax and it is quick like 25 minutes later i am home make n my self some food .A couple of burgers and some cheese and a pop to wash it down .now It is 1015pm now what do i do I feel like doing to much the pressure to think !I used to really like drives some times i would drive WEST or North But going west i would pick one road get on it and try to get to the End of the road! There is only a few that go to the state line .but Driving around and looking and seeing how people is pretty Good for the brain .And by time i am getting tried from driving i head for home and right to bed And i have learned how to help my self sleep after a day at work .Because some times days when it is bad from Weather or just a bad day get home and cant sleep sucks. Talk about dragging on .So i have learned something my self to do to help the body get charged up for the next day!A lot or times the next day is Great all ready to have done this for a few years Weight went to 225lbs and felt Great. And it is not funny when you put on a few pounds around the middle and you go to put your leg on and it is very tight walking is a little painful every step reminds you about the extra baggage. And then off to leg doctor to make the leg fit better. So i try to keep the same weight so it all works and weight lifting was hard to do at first because of keeping my balance is seriousness took me a few years again to work it out there is a lot but it hurts more when doctor say you will work it out. Like who do you ask about this?One thing i learned real fast don't tell any one about the spear tire you have on Then it starts more crap and you get treated like maybe other leg will just fly off and hit someone in the headland after all the years i still don't say much about it because of leg gone. I hate the after math to teach some one you are proud you can still walk like the rest. After being run over what has me puzzled is what am i suppose to say I cant do anything because my leg was chopped off. So sit in the corner and think Well i think differently I have to learn how to do things differently. But surly do something and work was a great step up the ladder .My leg was lost Aug 1983 was back to work Nov 17 1983 I was Happy as hell and this large company says we don't know what to do because you are the first amputee or disabled Like it starts again you have to teach them and tell them i want to work you figure it out let me know when you find the answer to the question. I will see you at work just look for the person who is smiling and happy and it seems to be real event doing all this at work i have had so many people ask why are you so happy just get laid ?No not yet but at work and like doing something to use my brain and body. you should try both it is nice feeling and walk away wondering maybe they kind of like fell on there head and can only use one not both parts of your body. I like walking away wondering they could have gotten hurt and don't know But me telling them the bad words amputee danger stay away !

This is worse feeling when Dr telling you sorry your leg has to go!You know the doctor is to help you. But what about the person working with you look at you like it i touch him his leg will come off. Spending time and your energy proving it is safe don't worry!And it makes for a long day ,Tell they have accepted you as is but as time goes and you get to say or hear a few jokes before you are part of the furniture. As this goes on and work kind of get you going I had something happen that kind of blew off my foot. One very Hot Summer Day I mean in the 90s and being at work had a good day,No rain or weather problems i was working a gate ares sweating real heavy as the realistic air lets you sweat real good and smelly as i was coming off the back of a 737 aircraft walking slowly looking up a little towards the terminal and seeing some real nice looking ladies and i can feel this large burning take place I look to make sure i see no orange /red flames or nothing but what is this from ?It is getting more and more now I am walking faster and faster time to get to wash room .I walk in to a stall but not sitting down lock the door almost rip off the pants as they fell to my knees i can see red stuff but this time it has some how shown down this new fiberglass leg as i see this i am getting real lite headed and like inner self steps in slow down you are okay sit down cool off and a few slow seconds go by i unstrap the leg and pull it up out of holder and blood is dripping as i pull it apart i am shaking don't pass out or panic .I have some paper towels i wrap around the stump and wipe up blood looking for the rip mark or opening !I found a good size one i know it is hospital time or doctors office i clean it up good bleeding has slowed down i put it back on i try to walk a few feet and lots of pain and slow burning i ask a boss .He is very uptight i need to go home or to hospital he asks why i told him i was bleeding pretty good !All of a sudden he stands up Lee you want a ambulance?I told him no i need to get this leg off and let it cool off so the bleeding stops. He sys Lee grab my shoulder he lifts me up off the ground and out the door we go He called the guy driving a van to get me to the parking lot. Now i know i will pass out but not from my leg but from the boss help picking me up he is 6'5"and 250lbs.As i was put in the van seat i yelled out Thanks as i was saying that he tells the guy Get me to the parking lot now don't waste time go !I have never seen this happen. Why is someone nice to me?I have never seen this happen before and it seems like about 21/2 to 3min pulling into parking lot and asks me where my truck is Bronco time,He pulls up close to mine i hop out open door and it was to late to say thanks he was gone!I dropped my pants and had this bloody leg off in seconds,drove to the leg guy he was close to work .He sees my leg and says you will be off till this closes up no work i will call work for you .Get home no leg on till i see you again in about 2 weeks I stay home on one leg and do very little to get this leg healed up and about 2 weeks later better and back to work i had to go to medical to get cleared for work no problem. So i try again until next time i made it and with work helps !

After being back to work about 1 hour feels great!Now i can get going and feel like the rest of the working class people,Even if i have a spear Tire on the left side .There is some things i have gone threw that still have no reason to understand. I was just home from work little messed up on the out side Bloody leg or not i have learned to make to make it by my self or not like being amputee i have learned to do what ever i can may be a little slower or different .But at least make it threw and at the part of life to see why or how. I had no real feeling of being any other way .If parents stopped fighting with each other and would think there is other human being in the room or house maybe they would not have enough time to fight and yell at each other .And at the same time care or show younger sons and daughters how to get threw life in one piece?And did nothing i was the one brother sister asked for help!I never stopped being Big Brother .Sometimes i had the answer and sometimes not But at least stay by them and help them on any thing possible and so called mother and father did very little .I belove this was what taught me how to make it one way or not. I was hurt so many time when i was a kid. Here is a good one for thought. As big brother runs the length of a barn on the roof And to jump off onto a large pile of straw .I learned to keep cool as i passed the pile of straw and still in the air .And to hear sisters and brother crying as i hit the Ground And sprain both ankles at once thank god i did not break both legs at once. I learned real quick The worse part was getting slapped by father and the remarks you want to learn how to fly!I will be glad to teach you asshole So i was home stuck on the couch or bed i stayed away from parents .But in your mind not knowing if it was true or not But not to treat my family like they did to me Would make sure of that these little events that happen as a kid would not go further there is life to this like now you see parents fighting each other or getting drunk what about the Great little kids in the same house what happens to them Well as i think of this it is a mold taken place you are making the shape to be used by lots and as it is used would it be better when a kid picks it up happy to use it and not get hurt. So the next time he or she awards for great thing they did learn for you not to see you in jail you have to build this mold for keeps and to last a long time .I till this day cant see why this is not important enough to do as grown up the past fights and fear stay with you in the back of that brain,Because i now have learned why when i was growing up had a very few friends and i am sure you can guess why?I will give you a hint at age 16 at 6'4" 175lbs and mad as a grizzly bear Can you wake up with finger marks on the inner part of your hands. When you close your fists and the marks are there when you wake up. Your eyes are not even open yet and very mad already. Well in case you cant believe it yes it did come from you as a person grown up in such a friendly home place yes this is the answer to your great parents who know it all. I thank God so many times to make sure i am not like them and the path to get threw it. And it is not that easy or peaceful. I will save it for later all i am doing is to make it threw the beat up side of your body getting better at work and a few years goes by Happy about work Glad i have made friends with my body with one leg short. I was to really love life and keep going happy as hell day after day !

And it is time to look into finding a partner!this sure will be fun to talk about why i have a shorter leg on one side and lots more .I wonder how i will feel doing this i think the words stress are due here it would be easer but that would be boring and am i really willing for the mental pain. Just work and worry about the rest later. You will know when to stop and get close to her or not maybe .And to show about the higher power stepping in and off to a nice real close partner. Forget about the bull but it does happen and i will need a tow truck to carry my smile it is to big past the ear to ear bull. It was so nice and accepted even it i have a half leg missing. One good part to start was traveling with a partner when you work with a large company time to go and the west coast beaches at sun down look great to see with a partner hanging on to our hand as walking down the shore line at the edge of the water ,Talking about just about anything on the brain waves is great feeling!I hope the rest of this going places is great as well as this one was .The large part about this leg is told and accepted no if and buts still sounds and talks like something is or could be worth something?Even a part of life as a young being is much a part of this. From my very friendly mother who is so nice like a very serious deadly snake. Every girl friend i went out with she would put in her two cents like what do you see in her?She is very ugly or where is her brains did she leave them some where else!Like she is rotten inside so i am suppose to be like her .No I will pass on that one. My talks or thoughts from mother was worthless again by my self and i have to make the answers to it all again myself. I would talk to so many friends would talk to me tell me how or what there parents might say. And nothing like the information i was told at home. Most

of my friends would say here is my keys to my car and some moneylender be home to late!One afternoon worked my mother 72 VW fastback when i was finished it was the best one ever seen not only a tune up washed inside and out tires polished every inch was shining spotless clean .I asked if i could borrow it to go out with who ever?Answer was no i an busy. I would say okay maybe next time and get don't hold your breath waiting. She would stay home watching TV So I would take the train to long island or bussed to queens very up tight to start and would ask a few weeks later to work on her car. Needs a tune up or what ever she would ask to do .If you want to use my car make sure it is done soon. None of my friends went threw it,Now i have learned to do it by my self and it seems may be i will have a girl friend soon. We both work at the same company We both work shifts that made it easy to leave early and be gone for the weekend. This went on for years nothing but smiles and good times Was so much fun walking around and made my legs stronger felt great very nice smile all the time.

' I look back now and thought i had it made being real Happy and content inside. Maybe time to be with her the rest of life. If it is this Happy and do so many things together i would really love to be a Dad and do this family stuff. This is first time ever this Good but Happy inside no more of this surface stuff. And only time frame i can put together is this very warm happy camping trip down southern Illinois is where it happen but nine months later first sons is here!Tyler William is about to be here come home from work one night on her day off She said you eat dinner you better take me to the hospital water broke!I think it is time I told her to hell with dinner How long ago did this happen she said about hour ago I helped her get coat on walk to truck and off we go to hospital and about 0700am time he popped out i watched all the good bloody slim come out as well gave out candy cigars happy as hell did it and learned a lot more than possible like no one from my side gave a dam m !It was two years when my mother called and saw him or even said anything about it all. I thought she is missing it is there problem And on her side all sisters mother any one came to see her and great looking Baby asap No questions about it and it got closer to her I thought as a son got on with it and i was home as much as possible i saw some events i was not sure about then and now it was right. She got very stressed out needed time to go shopping and get out with her sisters and mother .I said good bye have a good time shopping I had real close time with son doing anything i could like feeding him change his brown smelly diaper what put him in a car go for a drive he was out sleeping in about 30 seconds or less I would go home get him to bed and watch TV till she got in. Ask her how was shopping said just walked around mall never thought any thing was wrong and it was she was out doing what ever who knows. And we both fixed up our home more and more felt great had first son her and i close as possible soon after this she was back to work now we get back to doing camping and out doors things and Son was with us And can it be possible for this to happen one more time ?WE talked i told her we don't want son to be lonely and must have a sister and after a few very interesting times as always it happen again. But this time something was very wrong with her temper very nasty nothing like being in bed with a Grizzly Bear and huge fangs hanging out with some blood on the teeth part I had idea she was going to die or kill son And because she just was not all there. And it was hard to get to Doctors to see and when she come home from doctors she had a letter no more work and do little as possible but eating was there lots of it and she was very heavy in a short time But i hung in there took care of her she called me at work to come home to see her she was not doing to good i told i will be there asap what is wrong?She said after doctors telling her we will have twins she cant take it now!!!

I was not sure what she said so i asked her you and i are having TWINS together and you don't know what to do ?She said yes this is why I am so heavy and temper problems,I said so stay home do very little try to find something you feel like doing ,Cooking eating sewing anything you want to do!And don't worry i got it under control I gave her a large Hug tried to ask her if you need anything don't worry you have family Mother and sister Me your Son .What else could you want and it seemed to claim her down and just did that stayed home and when she told family all came to see her the next day to cheer her up and it did all was fine for a long time no problem at all so it seemed ?This was nine months of being messed with to the MAX !.I had been reading what to do to help her and i Did. But nothing helped she was rotten inside and was glad when this was almost over and even that was nerve bracken .Because she was put in hospital due to so much weight problem walking was to painful and her legs stopped working i was very shock up hoping her legs were okay after baby's are born and much more .But we will see. I was going after work to see her in the hospital bring her flowers any thing to cheer her up and got the call she was going in to the delivering room as i got there she was all strapped to a table .Doctors working on her one baby was born and one was tangled up inside so they had to go get him out with cutting her open .She asked me if i had the names for the boys(2) so now both names were done and no problem. But both sons were a few weeks early (3weeks) so they were kept ed in hospital for a few more weeks as well. So now i had a wife and three sons. I was really happy person loved it very much and i am nothing but a Father now and proud of it .And as it got going I had seen the very strange person who kept to her self unless you say or have money that seemed to be the most important thing Money,And as we got to the loud talks more and more one came out that i was not sure what to do ,But i did i thought was good to do and what she said she wants the Twins up for Adoption I felt like some one is about to screw up the family picture. No way not in my home will this take place. I kept my cool told her i will work midnights shift 10pm to 630 am in the morning no problem and i did it so she was home a short time with sons and the reason for this as i found out the sons messed up her way of being around .When she went shopping it was not but meeting people from work at his home or what ever and on my day off she was all done When i worked I bought the sleeping son in the full size van on the couch sleeping she would do was put sons to bed when she was home and do as she pleases when i get home at 645am she was sleeping would let me sleep till 1200pm noon she would go to work and not see sons till 845pm when she got home from work or put them to bed still sleeping from the van This is when she planned anything she wanted to do ?All i thought was how to take care of the family working around the house and cooking dinner with

his family and very much liked it all We were getting closed and closer
to sons and i did what ever we could do nothing like getting thrown
up by twins at the same time while out driving around .i was sitting
between two boys looking at each other one son let me have his lunch
back other sons saw what happen gave me back his lunch now i am
covered on both sides as i said pull over quick when she saw what
happen she laughs real loud ,We get all cleaned up and went home to
get some clean clothes on thank god for washing machines! This has
happen a few times but it really smells bad when you pick up your son
.Glad to see him hold him up in your arms are straight up and all of
sudden this brown smelly soup comes out all over the place .I walk
over to kitchen double sink put sons butts in sink in warm water I have
had it happen twice must be that twin inner feeling .This part of being
a parent no matter how smelly or sick the great little kids do to you ,It
gets much better and sooner the better. There were so many little event
like this happening i started to see something i was not sure of ?I know
i was very much watching wife and three sons .But it seems when sons
do something like get sick ,Fall throw up or comes out other end she
just sits there and watches,No maybe i am over protecting all of them.
I will watch and see as time goes by sons are walking getting around
i have noticed two of three sons follow me any where i go and when
they fall over or get hurt running they come to me to take care of them
.Now i am very much on the watch. Why are sons doing this i have
thought when i was a kid mother was the one who patched me up
from the road burns and the rips on the arms and knees. Father was
not home or would yell to go see your mother and that was it And one
little event took place that made me mad as hell One summer day the
grill was ready to cook dinner on couple of burgers smell real good I
walk away from the grill to go inside and get the buns for the burgers.
The sons are running around the back yard as i was walking back to
the grill i hear a loud scream and crying as i open the patio door I see
one son with both his hands stuck to the burning grill!I reach over
grab him he is yelling Dad I put his hands under cold running water
in kitchen sink .Now as wife is standing there i tell her get a towel and
put ice cubes in the towel as i am holding on to son who is crying and
yelling I try to claim him down now wife gives me the towel i tell son i
have to cover up his hands in the ice cubes you will feel better as i did

this he stopped crying but is laying his head on my shoulder i walk to my van put son in front seat laying him down with a seat belt hop in the van and off i go to the treatment centering is about 5 miles away i am going 60 MPH on my way and when i get to red lights i would look both ways not stop and keep going It felt like a matter of minutes and we were at center .As i grab my son pick him up walk as fast as i can inside Nurses walk up to me ask what happen grab him out of my arms and work on his hands ? As i sit in lobby let my heart slow down catch a breath or freethinking about this great little son with the nurses. And to make it worse i start thinking the actions if any that wife did as son was hurt!nothing was done by her did she panic deep inside And the one thought that is really aging me is she did not care?

all i can hear is I will stay here till you get back and watch the other two sons !As i wonder a little more the nurse comes over to me ask me where did i learn how to do as i did with my son?I said why ,because of your actions your son might not even have a mark or scare on his hands .You put his hands in ice right away was the best thing you can do!You did a Great job for your sons hands and shook my hands Nice job. And now my head puffed up fast great feeling to help your son or family member when this happens And a lot of bandages rapped around his hands,Put his head on my shoulder and i tell them thanks and out the door i go and back into van Son is all belted in leaning back and out he goes to sleep. I slow down driving take my time going home .As i pull into drive way Two sons come running out to see there brother and he is sleeping in front seat i pick him up and carry him to his bed lay him down ,let him rest a short nap he needs it after a day like today But where is wife what could she be doing in the kitchen cleaning up How is son doing went to bedroom to see him and another day i will never forget what happen So now i tell wife my turn to take a nap!I have to go to work tonight and this is Sunday night nice and quiet night about three hours later she wakes me up and get ready to go to work put on work clothes. I stop by sons all watching TV look at sons hands kiss him on the head and out the door i go to work. It will be a long night wondering how son is doing !

I have such a dull life. I really like taken care of three cute little dudes!I never thought i could do this and be happy about it!You see i am home doing same thing a mother is doing. But i am not peeled off the ceiling at end of the day. A small part i have not said a word about is work yes i do and i am happy about it And it is put on a second place with my sons i love to take care of .All of the time and a lot more demanding to do and for years it was work only. And if you wonder how much i do for work i will show you for a long time right now But years ago i was 18yrs old when i started i was full of energy and did not have much else to do with my self but can you think of some co worker who came to work on the forth of July and worked it was my day off. But was called at home to come in and work the holiday and 16 hours overtime on top of this .Yes i did do it and i did not fall down yet and hit my head .but they were short of people due to sick calls and called for help. I was still living home and told my mother I was going to work she asked me was i okay because of me going to work and what about going out the forth with friends. I told them i could see them later but making the bucks on overtime and i was glad i did get to work and it was slow as hell not much to do anyway. Great day and easy bucks .And when people at work asked me for what was i doing being at work stay home. And at end of day 20hours later i went home and i believe i was in a dream and out of it. Next day when i woke up i felt great i made it I was very much into my job. in case you are wondering it was a large company at the airport i am not suppose to say the name but lats say it was a large company .The reason is when you hear about the rest of a simple things that take place you will know why i cant tell you the name so i started in a large city better know for a big Apple. And working there for 4yrs was great after all this time Big Apple people work together and that is it no matter what .I am very glad what i was thought at a young age helped me for the rest of my time at work when i tell you this because you have supervisors who think they can write the laws about work and treat people like dirt and laugh at you as they go are in for a rude awaking in New York. I saw a event take place was great because a young supervisor yelled at people making remarks about a lady worker was put in place fast. Because his new Volvo 744 new gray car was torched before his own eyes. And replaced by a lady who was telling about her collage but could not

speak simple terms and was beaten to a pile of mashed potatoes quickly
and left as well and i learned when the company wanted something
done it was no question asked and it was done. I did not have a car
yet to go to work and after work i would take city bus and train back
to Brooklyn NY. Well after work I had to wrap my arms around my
stomach because of laughing so much it hurt when i took a step it was
a long trip home after work .. I was glad getting home this went on
for years laughing and having a good day at work and pay back then
was pretty good it was 510hr waggishness bad in 1973 min wage was
$1.85 hr before to long i have my First car 1971 Chevy super sport
454 four speed .Nothing but fun. I thought i paid a lot for it $2,500.
it had 38,000 miles on it .And i drove it on my days off from work or
took the train to work during the work week and it was fun. Any way
when you have long legs and don't mind walking to the train station
and back home this went on for years as well and it seemed just when
you get down packed there is a change in your picture. Now i get home
from work i lived in a large building in Brooklyn it was seven stories
up as I walk down the hall towards the apt. I see lots of boxes at my
front door as i get closer i see a piece of paper I pick it up unfold it
and read Lee you no longer live here any more Take your stuff have it
out of here by 5pm Mother !So now as the blood pressure takes off i
knock on the door but no answer!I walk out side and down the street
call some friends to come and help me with my stuff,and i move in
with a friend of mine who i grew up with same thing had to get out or
else !Not sure what to do now at least i still have a job ,What the hell
and a few more checks saved up and i will get my own apt .I hope sure
enough about three weeks later .One thing i like about payday it was
every week not every two weeks before pay check time .So on my days
off i find apt little place two bedrooms and rent is $145.00 a month it
took about a year before i had much to call home because all i had was
my stereo a car in the street and little bit of clothes and it was strange
because most to my friends came over to see me bought something i
could use in the apt. I had beds,couch,chairs table and a small dresser
.Told my friends thanks and today here it is 30 yrs later some of my
friends still call and talk to each other and i was in a so called accident
and a few of my friends were at the hospital to see me .and that was
about 1100 miles away to hospital ! So after about two years of this

apartment life time for a change. I had my brother living with me in apartment and we were bumbing heads and turned into fist fight were completely different people. I worked and did the best i could do and had friends at work .but my brother with all colors on his whole body from head to toeholds over the jobs like change over our shoes weekly and his answer to his low life jockey head out on the job. But i tried to help him being big brother i was 6'4"and 200lbsand brother was about 6'1"about 180lbs so to let him try to work I told him i had a plan and he was welcome to come along and he was real happy about it Go west young man and on Sept 1977 Good bye New York my brother had our apartment in boxes JFK airport air freight building and we took last flight out of New York 1130pm and 0630am San Francisco our new home and it was great place to live and play around so many great things to do it was worth it my brother and i went camping in the real mountains not like the hills up state NY and red wood forest is really super .I still think of it nice walking around and we had a few wines place to go to had so many free glasses of wine and about six months go by and my brother and i put on a few pounds cant see my ribs any more and more padding around the middle of course it has to change well at least i thought it did one morning about 0630 am i was driving to work on hwy 101 doing about 55mph and all sudden i cant keep my car in lane at this speed?As i look around out the window and see all the cars around me doing the same thing and all of sudden they all stop!Good Morning Dam m earth quake time and i had a cup of tea in my had I think it went out the window ?I have no idea what happen to it ?just as i catch my breath all the cars are moving again and up to 55MPH.But i am still shaking and cant hold on to the steering wheel so i pull over and stop the car get out as i open the door i try to get out of car and stand up like stretch my legs but not sure why i cant again it hits small earth quakes and i am on my way to work?After a few minutes it seems quiet so i get in the car and drive to work still shaking and my boss is telling me to relax it is the way it goes out here I look around and see people nervous all talking morning thing .No one said a word to me and it was a long day at work waiting to go home when the day is over ,I was glad to go home and relax i hope i make it home when i get home my brother is asking me how i am i tell him nervous as him and i cook dinner at home watching TV we both decide to go to sleep early we both get into our beds it hits again and this time i wonder because i know i had one beer with dinner but the bed moving and lights are off is someone else in this bed ?And short while later it is quiet again .Thank God for some sleep much needed after a day like today!

And now i have been in San Fran like after work going to the beech sitting down watching the sun going down But at work it is a mess and i really tried to help some co workers I feel because there English speaking was bad i feel the company was trying to pull something over them if they stayed over to finish up the job and patting them on the back and telling them thanks if it was a minute or two but when it is 30 minutes i believe it is overtime due to the worker to get paid for his or her work. And when the rule are about how long a person is on the shift and use his seniority to move around but they were moving people around as they wanted to and not by seniority .So i thought it was time to be a union rep to stop the people from getting the run around by the company .And i can say i wasted my time because then the company and the suck butt supervisor were following me around making remarks your from New York what is wrong with you ?I found away to keep them away was telling them my hands were getting so sore from fighting i needed a break and the sun was great they would walk away and not to say a word back it started again when the company had cops watching me search my car it was ripped apart looking for drugs or can of beer .I had a 1978 Chevy monza real nice and shinny after a special thing took place i learned a lot quickly real quick I feel i did the right thing but was told by union it was wrong to do what i did ?There was a lady worker who was close to my age like 21 or 22 yrs old very quiet nice to work with was going to collage to get some degree in art or something,not sure about it .but a person at work called co worker wanted sex actions with this lady telling her right there or in locker room making all kinds of remarks and the company did nothing about it .She asked if she could go home early and get away from this creep!And as always no we are short and i am keeping a eye on this guy because the girl is about 5'5" about 120lbs maybe and the creep is 6'2"about 175lbs no match for this lady and just as it happen I stepped in he had ripped this girls top open and bra was hanging all torn up as that happen she screamed i grabbed those metal trays that the cooks use like about 2 foot by 3 foot long and hit this dummy in the back of his head and he went down I stood there waiting to see if he gets up and i yelled call the cops and they did .It was a short time and they showed up and arrested him as they were going threw his locker found a pistol loaded and was busted and was not to come back to work !And up setting was union slim telling me i should not have done that to a union brother I asked union rep if he blasted them would he mind they walked away from me and that day in 1978 till now 2003 union would not say a word to me at all .I was wrong for saving this lady worker from getting who knows what could have happen ti her !And after doing that i thought was right to do I tried to reason this out with my self? like i am suppose to just look the other way while this person gets busted up and raped ?No i don't think so i am not a hero but enough is enough and wait till i tell you the out come of this after a day of this heavy stuff !I walk to locker room to sit down in a quiet place to catch my heart beat to slow down a little bit .I open the door lights go off as i step inside All i see is flying hand and feet hitting me in the back, shoulder, neck, and face. And i am on the floor now wondering what the hell this is about !And i cover up me head and hear feet going by me and down the hall way. I think it is over with i get up and go to wash room and look in mirror now and see lumps and bumps over my face and head,I walk to supervisors office as i get there he stands up asks me what happen to me ?I told him i walked to locker room lights went out and i was on the floor soon after. He says he will call the cops ?I tell him what are they going to do ?never mind the cops .I tell him i am going out side for a few minutes to catch my breath !He said go ahead watch out just in case ?I catch my breath a short while later and go back to my work area .All i do is keeping looking around my place and wonder who did this to me ?Nice place to work i was thinking better come to work with bullet proof vest and helmet?All of the fun is almost over close to 200pm time to go home .As i leave work i head for the beach to think things out !I sit in the warm sun And come up with a idea to do and make things safer for me at work?And next day at work i go see and talk with the manager. I tell him what happen and i want to get out of here and find a better place to work at !Next thing i hear is to go for a job interview out of state he tells me no job opening in New York .But half way home in Chicago is job interview?Great !And it is all set up on my day off i get on a plane for now and i am happy about it all !I have been here 10 months time to go and will not miss earth quakes at all!I have been marked a bad guy for helping a female co worker in need of help!As i get to Chicago and do the job interview i was given 5 days to get there for the new job !And i take my vacation time and packed up my car and tell my brother see ya out of here .He likes it so much and has not lost his job he will stay here With a Good luck and i am gone. As i drive by my self 16hrs later i am driving threw Chicago not to bad as i drive to the north west suburbs looking around found a apt not bad thanks to a co worker for his help!I like it better than San Fran All i did was work and sleep more and more and get to know the people here ! After working here 25 yrs and have a family with wife and three sons and nice home in a very nice place to live with school about three blocks away all of this picture seems nice after years of working and taken care of your family it all goes away with one quick event at work ?Sons are home sleeping wifes day off i go to work take my time driving .i work 10pm till 630am at a large building with plenty of other people as i was waiting for a co worker as we talk and read books so many times As he goes into wash room i wait out side the room for him so we can talk more about the books we were reading I have a can of coke in my hand As ground tractors coming in building and i was watching a worker going by me with a string of containers (4) coming by me i see a arm with something shining like a long rod hit me in the side of the head and i go down as the lights go out I am falling between Ltd-3 containers and over a yellow safety rail and towards the ground? I can hear workers screening and yelling as i fall as i hear the sound of bones snapping like sticks As it is harder to see it is all turning RED I can hear someone say call 911 and get a ambulance quickly!he is still alive .Now for the long line of fun and lies are about to start?And 61/2 minutes later i am at the hospital and a bloody mess as well. As i talked to the ambulance driver 4 yrs later that is how long it took to find them but was told some more things about the mess i was in they gave up on me because with the brain hanging out and blood all over the place they thought i would not make it ?And i was given 7 units of blood in the ER to keep me alive and what is was told by doctors as well as in writing they don't know why i am still alive and kicking?What they found was two blood clots one in front of head and one on the side but seven holes put in a one inch area of my skull behind my right ear? Doctors said i was still alive again because my blood was very rich no drugs or alcohol being put into a body cast due to so many broken bones like arms,leg, hip ,ribs and skull in many pieces as well. Thank God still alive when waking up days later and see wife But have no idea who kids belong to as there are my sons and could not talk right words were all twisted up and together what a way to talk but it gets better down the line It took months for the words to get better and talk real wordplay other part i hated was tubes every where both arms leg nose and a few more place ?you name it and there was a tube there!Asked nurse when i was going home and was told don't think about it you have a ways to go ?And not being able to hear right or smell a thing really is the pits!Doctors said i have to learn how to talk and put my memory back together before anything happens. Nurses ask me what happen i told them i don't have any idea? So now i have to get better from the inside out to go home !no problem just put it all where i need it to get some where .I was set up in classes to learn how to read again as well as talk that was hard enough but having double vision for about 21/2 years and i don't drink any beers reading was getting better but could write my own name fingers did not work to good just as i start to get better the lights go out and the nerves in my head pop apart and eyes stop working next morning in surgery and i had a shunt valve put in back of head to help with the pressure in head .but still had double vision for years till it went away now it is the end of October and the trees are bare out side and i wonder when i am going home ?Now i am back in classes to learn how to read and see better .As a worker comes to see me pretty messed up pretty good as we were talking a special jerk from work come and asks me questions on the so called accident i told him i have no idea he said glad to hear that it is your fault you stepped into moving tractor ? and leaves after telling me the lies that happen at work ?Can you wonder at shift change and no one say a thing ?Sure i was told by a few people workers were told to stay away from me or they will be next to get hurt or killed?As my friend heard this jerk say this about me walking into moving tractor and cant believe it .He is the same jerk who said he asked 36 workers if any one saw anything happen to me ?as my friend from work leaves this really messed me up all i can hear is this person say i walked into moving tractor. Sure can you think and chew at the same time ?After loosing my leg on a motorcycle accident don't you think you become more aware of things around you ?No so i am into pain and walked into a 6,500lb tractor for fun. sure and this event was not my fault ??   Have no idea of who or what hit me but still have memory of seeing a long are with a silver rod hitting me in the head and putting me down .As i am trying to get better a doctor asks me questions every time he see me and the numbers he tells me i still cant remember back to tell him But am told by doctors it will come back but takes time as your body and skull get better so will your memory!And in a matter of time i hear a tractor going over me and the sound of my bones snapping really bothers me as the same noise of people screening in the back ground at work !and for a long time all i try to do is think about the cause of all the injury to my body and to be thank full piece by piece slowly it starts to come back and after 5 months in the hospital i get the chance to go home at last,thank god still alive and kicking.but something is wrong as wife not saying much to me on anything .like i had a head trauma now i am the bad guy!as we were driving home not much talking but three little sons happy as hell i am coming home at last have to use a cane to walk with being so out of balance and don't drink Soon i hope but glad to get back to work have a little jar of medications to take for a while. Was only home a short while and off to hospital ER with very bad headaches call migraine time was being shot up with medications and sent home as wife was getting pissed at more and more. A few times had a ambulance take me to hospital due to headaches real badminton home 2 weeks now and have to start going to school again to learn to read as well as talk i was going to school i had doctors pull me out of class headaches are so often and so bad .But instead of class i start seeing a real doctor to help me with third head injury stuff and get to talk about it as well. As this doctor knows a lot about this head injury and how to help you threw it as well Doctor Hill i will keep it short to make sure no one will bother him about this writing or information on me as well?And he was a great doctor stopped the headaches as well as the pain was so bad and did as he said and what to take no problems . even helped with the great day i made it back to work with his helping made sure i got better and faster and it worked   and after talking with DR H he tells me to start writing down what happened at work or what i remember and it all helps put the picture back together as well as think about it and not get uptight with thoughts about it With his help reading the hospital paper work on this event helped a lot to understand what they did to keep me alive but as well as read what doctors found on my body when i was pretty mashed up. And where to go to find out more information about it as well but no police reports missing?And a lot more that the company did to make sure no one will tell you a thing,One low life cop i talked with said i cant tell you a thing about it have a good day i called him some names to his face at a cop shop what a full size puppet and it does not stop there even the lieing FBI puppets said it never happen and was told i would be arrested if i talk about it .But the sad part is going to 27 lawyers about this event and being told sorry but the lieing company will do or lie to make sure no one knows a thing about it !After that and being told that i tried congressman and was told man bad accident be glad to help you but what is name of company, sorry cant help you good by!After all of this i go and talk with doctors who put me back together little by little ask them about this and being told not accident and in writing injury to head not accident related body injury secondary?Nice to live with back to DR H and reads it and fills me in as a doctor writes form hospital about the seven holes on right side of skull he also is the doctor who measures the seven hole diameter and how deep into the brain they went and all in a one inch area behind right ear!after he wrote it came from ice pick or board with a nail in it i wonder how the jerks at work try to say i walked into moving tractor ??But there is one small part that i wish would happen but will not Due to lieing company track record?But when i was hit and put down i was a few feet from VHS cameras right over my head looking right where i was standing when i was hit in side of head and put down but more out of place is the jerk who came to hospital and said it was my fault is the only person with the key to the room with all the recorders tapes?But for some reason my tape is missing i wonder who did it ?And to fill you in on strange events after being run over with the tractor and two carts it was put in a chained up area for reason unsure about but some how it turned up missing as well ?But they came to hospital and said it was

my fault?sure maybe they will buy the Brooklyn bridge cheep on sale ?
All of this is taken place it get worse inside because start having dreams
so bad afraid to go to sleep three day at a time to much noise and
sounds from this so called accident!When that starts i start having
more and more memory of it and see the picture of thing like tractor
going over me noise from screening of co workers who i used to work
with ?the sound of ribs snapping with the sound of your hip crunching
noise And before long shaking so bad have bitten my own tough so
many times blood all over the mouth! thank god for Dr H he tought
me how to make peace with this before i snap and end up in a rubber
room This was going on so many times .I would be sleeping out cold
and wake up yelling out loud it was so bad i was afraid to go to sleep
and hear this .This is what i go threw but i have found a way to breath
and sleep better and not think of this as much that is why i call it make
peace with it !and if you think that is bad to go threw it is only the
start of a turned up life only home a matter of weeks and to see wife
put hand and foot threw wall yelling for me to get out of house that is
just a start?But now at work the playing mind game is worse because
the facts from workers as well as the games from the company is worse
and you learn how to do more !First not to let it bother you and keep
going no matter what it is .Went threw this divorce thing after being
sent by lawyers to have your brain checked out to make sure it still
works no problem just keep your cool no temper matter or you are
done before it starts I was at a rehab place when hit with some much
bull like don't come home stay there we will talk about it bull nothing
till i was back at work .So i found a place to live and do it by my self
but sons loved coming over no problem and was taking sons to the zoo
,parks,slot car places you named it we went to it so i could keep my
sons happy and i worked well as she was made to see sons having a
good time and not much long it was taken out on the sons they were
being kept home not allowed out no friends etc But the greatest happen
when sons took a cab to my house and waited for me to get home
from work went to cop shop with papers from cab sons called and
took,without me doing a thing about it after talking with sons by there
selfs to find out they wanted to be with dad and not mother is the way
to start the battle and it did happen for a long time And i got the last
laugh the sons were now with me and done!so now one down and one

to go work and there games was a real mess with nothing but lies lies and more lies from the company as i kept it all in writing every day at work not matter what did or did not happen to me by them! Now as the work place starts following you around with remarks like whats wrong with you you had a head trauma whats wrong with you brain damage! this is along with every pay check for 8 months missing one hundred or two hundred dollars till i go to pat roll mad as a snake and start yelling then no problem and no more check problems Even when i bought court orders and was told by payroll dept we don't have to follow the court order and threw the papers on the floor till a judge was told of there game being played no problem all taken care of !Now there is more problems that are very hard to be cool but you are labeled brain damage and are not suppose to be able to think or talk !When you keep your cool and talk make sure it is in writing so more people can see there actions againist you and they loose To see what i mean here is one a supervisor tells co workers not to talk or work with me because of pending charges!After i told them about this and more charges filed against them again but the looks from the workers like you are going along with this as well sorry i don't have sucker stamped on my head And to tell the doctor of there actions that is being done to you is hard as well even the doctor asks question like what is wrong with these people all i wanted to do was work ?And due to these games and not to get mad i used to takes walks all the time to relax and get the blood pressure down and not snap !There are days i never said one word to any one person nothing to say to people you cant trust!And to make it worse and you did nothing wrong a few time Doctor H pulled me from work and here is why you are happy you made it back to work feel human again after all the fun but work puts you right back to where you were hurt you ask to be moved but is told sorry we cant do that?So you keep your cool and work the best you can but before to long you are shaking and feeling bad call the doctor and are told to go home !now you feel bad after this but doctor tells you why you feel bad and are shaking and it gets more rotten that night you try to go to sleep but wake up yelling ,because you are in a accident again or not sure now it is bad dream time from being in the same spot you were put to work in but all you did was work but the problem is you are still thinking about the accident and have not made peace with it yet and have very serious thoughts on it more and more Even after your doctor write a letter telling them to move you out of there and are not moved!Time to stay home for 11 months till it stops eating at you and you start to sleep again longer time frames and not 2 or 3 hrs and up shaking and yelling in pain? All of this because you had a head trauma and are not suppose to know about it more bull on the way sorry my doctor put me back together to live and not be a worthless person ! this has happen more than once and the very some thing happen when i get home for the last time and wife cant stand you wants divorce so you live with a family member in another state out west you feel great weather is very mild warm and not muggy you slow down on pain medications feel great sleeping is 8 to 10 hrs which is really good and a few pounds on in the middle doctors say you are doing great then it starts first a letter from insurance people saying move back or else a few days later you get a phone call from same people who wrote you that letter But now you are told move back to the state you were hurt in or your insurance will be stopped so now after 4 months of doing great you have to go back to the mess place in 14 days or else,no insurance coverage ! Now i am all packed up and ready to get back to the place where i was hurt and not to happy about it all !As i am driving and thinking about this whole thing why do i have to go back and maybe they will help me get back to work sooner we will see the fun soon about 16hrs later i am back looking for a place to live i start calling people i know to see if they know of where to live at and the second person i called said his town home was empty and no problem moving in and told me how much to pay for rent fee great no problem i hop back in van drive to town house not to far away and he is there i unload my stuff and i made it again and happy i did it again no problems and this was on the weekend come Monday morning i called insurance people and let them know i was back .but i asked them about going back to work no problem once i get cleared So after all this time off when i go to company medical to get cleared for work i tried not to laugh to loud in there faces?But am asked what am i here for?I tell to go back to work and was told you look fine to me and signed the from return to work no restrictions i walk out think i had to do all of that to go back to work i wonder if he is a real doctor ?As i get to the supervisors office and hand them the from they tell me to start on Sunday morning no problem!now i walk away as head puffs up and i thought i will make it again and i did and will try some more !lets see how long it will last this time around .And i was back to work one day and put in for different jobs again maybe i will get out of this place and we will see what happens ! and about two or three days later i was called for job interview so i go no problem take the walk around and all the talking and was told we will call you soon with a job reporting date !So now i have my chin up knowing i will be out of here soon this is just before spring rush startup something is wrong now as six months has come and gone still there with the old job place. So i call the people and was told to come and take a test again and start over with the job interview?Why now what i go there on my days off and do the test and all the talking no problem again i am told we will call you next for the job!now it has done it again now a year later and nothing and they hired off the streets and from different dept but not me ?So i call same person again and told you have to take a test again and you did not talk enough last time about the job!I call people i know in the dept and am told just what i did not need to hear and don't see what the run around is but they told me i was next to be hired no problems i tell them thanks call people about jobs dept and was told no you are not hired next you will have to wait and see ! As all of this is going on pain in the body is getting more and more ,And as the sleep at nights gets less and less down to about 2hrs sleep or no sleep at all I would just go to work and do the best i could as i keep going hoping for better days to come .I am used to not talking with many if any people at work this has been going on for a long time .and that is why i just do my job and not say much else about any thing It is a long day at work but i just hope for the best and i cant give up yet for any thing !This is why going and talking with a great Doctor H is the way to get threw this and to learn and be told i am not the bad guy All i wanted to do is get on with life after this accident cover up .And just as i start to get used to waiting i get called from medical dept from the company they want me to go to medical and see some doctor they?I try to ask for what and was told you will see when you get there!So off to medical dept i take the company bus there walk in sign my name wait to be called and see what happens next?And in a few minutes i was called to go to the room and wait for the doctor?Now i am puzzled as hell about the reason for this but i just do as told and go along with it!Doctor comes in same one who cleared me to return to work asked questions how am i doing how do i feel after telling fine i am okay i was told see ya next time and walk away get on bus back to work area thinking what a waste of time and questions what a joke to be playing on a person who wants to work and get on with it !this happen a few times in a row,as i tell my doctor about this My Doctor says he want to meet and talk with the company doctor to help understand about the Trauma i have been threw I thought that was a great way to get the people off my back and they would know more about this medical stuff i went threw!I was so happy driving my Doctor to work in my van i thought it was really nice for my Doctor to spend his time trying to help me out and see what can be done about this whole mess. And i do mean mess about to get worse! As we pull up to the guards shack i get out to see what i have to do to get my Doctor H threw it But was told by Guard they will call medical and have the company come and gets us!So i hop back in to the van and tell the Doctor we have to wait for medical to come and gets us!And in a few minutes i see the company doctor pull up i hop out and walk up to company doctor just about Hello and the yelling started from company doctor tell me how dare you for bring the Doctor here to talk to him he is not talking to him and will see me get fired for bring him here as well. I tried to tell him so the Doctor can explain the medical trauma i went threw and what to do about because you said you cant read his letters .He walks away gets in to his car and drives off not saying another word !As my Doctor waves me to come on lets go So as get in start up the van my doctor tell me don't worry he cant handle a real Doctor don't worry about you will be okay. As i drive the doctor back i fell real bad try to do something and no good .Now i wonder what will happen next to me at work,What will they do to me next as well?I did all of this on my day off as i drop the doctor i thank him i cant believe he did all of this and was told no problem see ya soon!I head for home wondering all the way what will happen next And a few minutes go by and i am home i get to the bed room and lay down like a matter of seconds later the phone rings and yes it is medical yelling at me for bring in the doctor and i was told they will see me soon at work and talk about this little mishap!I tell them i just tried to let a real Doctor talk to them because they said they cant read what the doctor wrote about ?And as i was finished talking they hung up Now talk about feeling bad and down the dumps after this i thought it was for a good reason not this after words And i have work tomorrow this will be interesting day coming up !And i was thinking they cant fire me what did i do wrong ,nothing just stuck in the middle man is that the pits !

As i am still home wondering about next thing it starts getting dark out and a short while later it is pouring out side raining real hard out and the pain in hips and side of the head are real bad i have plenty of med to take and try to relax and let the pain ease up And i fall asleep for about 40minutes and it helps little to relax after that little sleep It helps. I call my Doctor and tell him about the call i got from work and was told don't worry about you are doing okay .Trying to get something done and all i want to do is work And my body was tore up so bad and not from a accident and the company knows it was not accident as well but are playing dumb !They have done such a nice job covering it up after years of practice doing something like this like you are not suppose to know about it And why i say this is after going to OSHA and talking to the person who came to work and took pictures of the area where you were hurt and tells you about the company track record and the long list of doing this so many times and for so long But you are not suppose to find this out you had brain trauma and are suppose to be dumb , Or very slow!Well i have Some news for you sorry kiss my shorts !I have done more things to get on with work with life And have pieced more about this cover up by my self I have to because a few words my these Tie jockeys You walked into a Moving Tractor!Bull bull and more,(LIES)There is a part still coming to the part of the brain called thoughts. I have said it so many times I still remember seeing a hand with a silver rod hitting me in the side of the head And a few more parts like the door next to the end of the wash room or the right side is a heavy steel door that can only be opened from the other side but when you are going down after being hit and you hear that door close it makes a special noise as it stops and hitting the steel frame ?Why is that taken place and moving and closing !There are a few more things that have happen that you know i did not do And here is another one And you don't have to do much to see about this lies and cover up But i was standing and waiting for co worker to pop out of wash room so we can talk a little more before shift starts AS i was drinking a can of COKE and leaning on a yellow rail in front of wash room No big Deal Then how and why was my bloody ass found behind the was room under the safety rail ?I asked the paramedic who picked up my bloody butt and was told same thing was found behind wash room ?If i walked into moving tractor what was he doing driving into wash room and pulled a u turn Sure!Another lies by the company But the answer to many thing is when i talked with the Doctor who put my skull back together as he also looked in the Seven hole that went threw my skull all in a one inch area on my skull And just in case you think that is sick he also measured how far into the brain they went and put down the depth of each and every hole in my skull in writing and not to easy to read about as he wrote injury to Head not accident related ?I would like to see how many people can live with that event in there mind wondering what the hell is this about and why?Soon after i found out that information i was getting calls at home that the puppet jerks FBI taped and knew who was doing it but did nothing about it ?But when i go and see one FBI person he tells me keep a gun around they will try again because you are still alive !And in the back of my head all i want to do is work !And because we are talking about the lies from some tie jockeys that really are low life worried about me a few thing happen with them !one i called told him about this accident is one who told me any problems come and see me so after i called him tried to set up a day to talk with retired in a matter of seconds after the call But his sectary called me asked me what did i say to him because he did not tell any one he was retiring asap!I wonder if he is the one who helped cover up the Gun shipment that was missing when i was hit and put down?Na he retired forget about it ?"Another bit of information from FBI was he said wife changed insurance coverage days before this event ?So call the insurance people and he was right and the coverage was upped amount ?But after it happen they will not do a thing about it ?why $$$$$$$ So many things like this happen where ever you go trying to find out information is unreal. I Go to the city police dept trying to get the accident report what a mess after filling out the paper work and questions about this matter the lady asks me am i sure about this because there is nothing on file about after i show her the marks on my head she steps back and looks at me strange and says sorry there is nothing But when i ask for help from a Great Congressman and he has a whole pile of papers about this you want to go back to the cop shop and throw up i there faces and tell them there is none! and see what they do or say next ?After doing all of this to put something together about this matter i get tired of the games being played on me from work time to start more fun!EEOC and start the charges to see the out come what a mess as well,Remember NO GUTS NO GLORY !! AS i am real quiet about all of this the feed back is unreal The low life supervisor who tell you and play games on you about this event that has happen now are more a pain and talk nothing worth it at all T Hey tell this never happen and i am so mess up and don't know what i am talking about ?Only I talk after talking with the Doctors who kept me alive

and know what happen or the cause of the injury to the head and body!I went to the cop shop by work who were called when this happen and the paper they wrote on was blank ?After tracking them down and asking questions and would say a word to me, but have a nice day I called one some names right to his face in the cop shop and walked away nothing happen ?Now you know they were taken care of by some one ?You try that some where else your butt will be in jail!I just give up and go home what a waste of time to do this and get no where! This really does a job on your brain now you wonder why or what did i do to get this way!Because so many people who are in this story or picture will not even talk to you?This is like never ending and no answers to get anywhere!And get something off your brain it would help dreams of being hit and put down are very hard to settle with or make peace with it to get it off of you and your thoughtfulness is a part i have not said much about due to there do nothing ways and only what the company said goes what a waste of time and money as well because after this event they wont say a word to me about anything they know they may get there butts kicked down the street real soon and no witness?just like they do 30yrs of they waste of time but closed shop and you have to have union coverage what a joke to deal with! As i am dealing with all of this work matter just to make sure i did sleep i am fighting for three special great sons and that is just as bad after being sent to doctors to make sure i am a good Father as well as a person the games from that is just as bad And i hurts just as bad or more when sons call you want to see you and you have to get a court order or what ever just to see your son after a while of this you get real crabby fast Like the two low life's are fighting to make you life as rotten as possible you have work and the tie jockey games and ex wife with the mind games and you wonder which one is the worse and it seems a tie to me both are trying to get you to snap ,Sorry no way cant give in to the low life's just so people see what low life's do to you watch this You are back at work sitting with doing to do sit at your desk and go threw computer looking at weather news not much else just in case,you don't even get a call for hours at a time this happen on a sat .pretty quiet you take your walk and back and not much else as not even the other workers talk to you they were told to say away from you do to the EEOC charges,But one call comes in and it is your son tell you one son fell on bike and broke his arm and can you come home to get him to the hospital and the punch line this is the seventh time your son called and was able to talk to you he was cut off?So i ask supervisor about going home to get one son to the hospital ?And to be told no we are busy you have to wait till it is time to go home ?I try to tell him son fell and broke arm but it meant nothing So i told son to have the neighbor take him and i will get there asap Son i now not to happy about me not there to help them but i have to sit and do nothing till time to go home about 3 more hrs So i some how keep my cookies in the jar and wait and to make it seem funny i did not have another call till i even went home nothing sit and do nothing as your son is hurt !What a classy place to work !You have to keep your cool man is that hard or what . As i drive home as fast possible to get home and get to sons side i do and sure enough he is in bed with his arm up on pillow and nice clean cast!The other sons came in nice and quiet and told me how he fell off his bike with arm busting as he hit the ground hard and fast !I get the last laugh any way i am off tomorrow i will stay around home and keep eye on sons any way !And being home i thought was great because raining out real bad pain is pretty bad might have gone home from work any way But today sit and take it easy .and about 0930 am i get a call from FBI talking about this work event and being told sorry we cant help you is the pits So to make it even worse every one i have gone to not one person will or can do anything about this so called accident what a joke You are not suppose to get upset and let anything bother you !sure I is very hard to wonder who tried to kill you that is bad enough but now it seems no one will do a dam m thing about But if you fart the wrong smell your ass will be in jail asap or sooner as you have been told so many times by FBI and the cops and don't let this bother you at all ?After sitting for a few minutes in shock the phone rings again now what i answer now the work medical dept says they want to see me tomorrow at work again?I tell okay see you tomorrow when possible from work area and they said 10am be there don't worry about your work area i said okay see ya later Bye!And today is my day off what a day already As this is all going on you wonder what the hell is this and why no one else has done this and laugh about it but every where or any thing i do i have the eye looking around and you wonder like you have been told so many times by so many people watch out they will try again to kill you How do you relax after all of that in your mind running around over and over!It has its toll because you don't leave anything unlocked like truck doors house doors or anything there is it is all locked up just in case and when you have two or three dogs as well to help keep eye on anything or any one around you they bark and you go looking why or where it came from ! And you don't put the guard down for a second at all

As all this is going on with the thought of it happening again you wonder as well, when,where that is always on your mind as well part of the guard taken place All you want to do is work and keep the mind off the past and to keep going but so many things on you,You get some re leaf when talking to Doctor because most people have no idea of what you are going threw or have been threw. And not to let it get to you as well Keep on going !This is like i have already gone threw 27 lawyers and not a one will do a thing about this little pile of bull and there is a few answers why it is so hard to sleep wonder why ?I will try to go to newspapers call them next and see what can be done about all of this So in the morning i start calling l of the paper places and No Good we don't do that company about this or anything i try news stations as well same thing they cant because company will no release information to prove a thing? and makes you wonder again this is

America do as you please what a crook of you know what ?Now i go back to congressman's office and try to ask for help from them,to see if maybe us dept of justice will step in and help with this as well So `now i am told you will get a letter and we will see what can be done if anything is possible .After about hour talking i thank him and head for home and wondering whats next .As i get home sit down sons are coming home from school i make some snacks for them to eat and get the brain off of today and just think about sons and how they are doing !after they are done eating i ask if they want to go to the parks and we are gone in seconds we all walk together in the parks following the trails around looking as we go at all the trees and creeks what ever and it is very relaxing to do and feels great we are all out walking around for about 2hrs and head back to the van as we are getting closer to home i pull in ice cream place and sons eyes all watch and look for what they want to eat and a matter of minutes we are all sitting and eating ice cream and take our time ! Short while later we head for home about half way home it is very quiet i turn and see all the sons sleeping on the couch next to each other And once home i get them into the house right to there beds it is almost 9pm time for Them to be sleeping anyway !And i go lay on the bed thinking about the fun i have had the last few days with Doctors ,lawyers,cops,work people what a week I work for a few days of same old stuff no one talking to you and sit and do nothing for 8hrs is along day!I drive home in the afternoon and just make in home before sons come home from school they grab the mail for me on the way in to the house .Sure enough letters from the govt i ripped open and start reading what a letter note enough reason to do a thing sorry about the cause of accident!Call congressman ask him to fill me in on the letter he has as well. He says he cant believe nothing to be done about this mess at work. How does this happen this is not a accident but it does not matter what i say ?I know i am speaking English words but is does do matter you can almost get killed at work due to this strange actions taken place and it is like so what !You even have more and more memory of this and to get that across to a person who speaks English is worthless And wait till the rest of this is out and it is very close to the same way it is all forgotten about and again from the good old government the same old stuff?What do you do throw it away ,no it is your life that is being played with all you did was work and work well better then most ever will even try to do So. to draw you a little seen to this event here goes !There is a few different govt departments that are A.D.A. and E.E.O.C. and few that work with disabled people and some that make sure laws are followed and and few more but to get any type of help or support from them you better stand on your head and sing !once i called ADA tried to explain to them about what had happen at work and it met nothing call us dept of justice i have enough letters from them to make enough wall paper to go from here to pol land in different colors You get all the letters from the congress sent and the idea they may look into it but never happen when you write them you get a letter back in few days sorry we cant help you better off sucking a dozen raw eggs you might fell better than getting there paper work back ,Good old worthless Just so you fell better like what the fudge do you do to get them off there chair warmer and at least take a look into any part of this cover up !So after some of this .And what i learned as part of this was to get it all in writing all you do is tell who ever you are dealing with ,Look i have memory problems can you give me it in writing so i don't forget it?The letters you get will help with these people EEOC they will tell you any proof of what was done to you Sure it is in writing you cant get the job because of your disabled or we wont transfer you due to your being disabled I had a few of them it helps the charges you filed to prove what happen and the company cant say you did not happen to due to the letter with the problem in writing and you win But there is a catch to this when you win a few charges and told by EEOC it is worth so much dollars you feel better for all the run around and the dieing company wont go near you again But the problem is when all the charges seem to disappear and even the judge looks at you kind of strange like where did they go !But you call EEOC and they tell you sorry your charges are still on file Now which one is it ?And when the EEOC person leaves the job after so many years you wonder how much did they get ?It happen twice And one nice person from EEOC tells you they came into a lot of funds and to not from the lottery or family but i cant tell you the company name sorry !Now what do you do ?I learned to say a pray every day maybe a bolt of lighting will hit the dieing person sooner? All around is money you sign to settle for a good amount but it turned up missing the company tell you the sooner you sign for it the sooner you get the check and after you sign for it it is missing and the lieing company says we never did it ? Try living with all of this ?All i can think is you hear about people going to work and loosing it wonder why or how?And you have people come up to you and ask why you don't smile or laugh ever think there back side is hurting bad enough form the company games!So today at work i have to go to medical for the talk what a joke . but i will play along and see what happens next As i am driving to work wondering what will we talk about at medical depth worry about it later nice day out i will think about it later .once at work i tell the supervisor i am on my way to medical see you later ,Get to medical dept have a seat and a matter of a few seconds i am called to walk back and see the doctor i sit down again and he pops in asks how am i doing no problem pain is the same work is okay ?I get back glad to hear that you take care see you next week ?off i go back to my work area and do nothing much!I have all the papers from the accident with me to make copies and keep them nice and clean but i get a call from the boss of the work place and he is the boss of the whole operation he wants to talk with me and see how i am doing So now i walk the length of the building and go upstairs to his office .He is waiting for me as i try to talk to him about this ?i try to tell him this is not accident as well as about the cover up as hid jaw hits the floor what i have told him he asks to read the paper work and get back to me the next day?So i leave them and walk back to my area .next day around lunch time i go back to the office and try to talk with him again what a waste of time and air!does not matter what i have said as well as what the paper work says i get no this is not right sorry this did not happen where you were work sure you did not walk into tractor and don't remember what happen ?I tried to tell him what i remember about being hit and put down and the gun shipment missing as well .But no that did not happen sorry cant help you you take care and watch out what you are doing !I just walk away mad as hell thinking another sucker and waste of time . I did not tell any one i talked with this jerk and went back to my area and soon it was time to go home i leave very fast and not a word out of my mouth once in my van head for home and i start to relax heart slows down not angry any longer nice day almost home i stop at a hardware store to pick up some things for sons bike and guess who is in the store ?The jerk i just talked with early in the day i walk up to him say hello he steps back like i was going to slap his ass and looks at me strange, you can see the fear in his eyes and says hi what am i doing here i show him the stuff and walk away he just stands there and is waiting for me to leave he store !I get to van and watching the store he has not come out yet i drive off real slow and i see him get out and walk to his pick up real fast .but he goes the other way towards town like i was going to follow him home nothing better to do sorry not this time i have sons to take care of sorry !What a waste of time and he is the boss of the whole place and every thing going on he knows about first .What a wimp! and if you think i am kidding next day at work his sectary calls me asks me what did i say to him i asked why i just told him what i had done to me at work .She says he retired and is gone not coming back Like i said what a wimp !And to say more he had a brother who worked there he retired the same way is gone as well and no reason why to any one ? So here is another person who knew about this accident and they left as well three down and a few more to go But all of this fun has me messed up real bad migraine headache time and my balance is real bad i have trouble walking and cant pick up my head it hurts to much and the pain all over body is pounding away at me i ask the supervisor if i can go home and he says good bye you don't look to good whats wrong ?I told him about headache and i went to the van tried to drive to the hospital i did but pretty slow on the far right side of road as i only have to go a few blocks and there once there i tried to walk to the ER as i get into the hospital room they grab me put me in wheel chair and ask me whats wrong no problem i was put in a room and the lights were turned off and shortly a doctor came in gave me a shot and said try to sleep for a short while and i was out 45minutes later wake up and all gone fell pretty good but moving slow and real easy just in case i had t sit in a area for about 30minutes to get the nerves to claim down once that happens i get up and get to my van and drive home nice and easy all the way home .once home i tell sons i went to hospital and they said Dad you go rest we will be okay i tell them thanks about hour later feel real good and rested up ready to go .as sons were all watching TV and doing home work i cooked up dinner and we were all fine talking about the day at school !We all sat around watching movies till 9pm time to get to bed for the sons they helped me clean up and all of us

with?And that is why he keeps asking me if a remember anything about the accident ?And on top of that he was the only one driving in the rest either went home or did not get started yet   As i talk with the Doctor i tell him about the idea i have about who might be the one who ran me over?he says it looks like it am right And another part is the door closing that goes down stairs from the different dept .Only they are in and out but all have gone home already no one around from that dept now or when i was hit and put down why was the door closing fast and loud,I still hear that sound steel on steel noise!The other part is the missing tape would show it may have been going threw the door and down the stairs?And maybe if the FBI knew it as well may be they could look into it as well Doctor says it wont hurt to try and see what happens about it. The doctor tell me about the skull of mine in pieces and some of it was left open to let the brain go down in size after it is all puffed up from so much damage That is part of why i was kept out till the brain goes down in size as well Man does that sound sick or what !cant see a person with a puffed up brain it sounds sick but scary how it could happen to a person!That is part of it the other part is my body was puffed up as well all over the place And lots of black and blues from head to toe?After a another great talk with Doctor hill says thanks And out the door i go and head for home There is this deal sons and i have they wait at home till i get there before they take off to friends or any thing else .As i am driving and no wood burning brain is still thing about what i was told from doctor H it is so great to under stand what was done to me in English i know some times why i was given so much blood threw the IVs And why the coma was done to me ?I helps a lot to know about this .it helps a lot May be this is why i cant give up ?Not sure why or how but alway keep going NO matter what just to get a few answers would help a lot !As i learn more and more the answer i have come up with more and more and you can see the proof a lot clearer i did not step into moving tractor! As all of this is taken place more and more it makes you wonder how can a scummy company get away with lie after lie to cover there smelly butts is a wonder ?This is suppose to be AMERICA land of home and brave what a bunch of suck butts with ties on ?And i wonder you had to go to collage to learn how to lie and be a suck butt?But to make it even worse there supervisors are even low to the sewer then them I have had some good times with a few brainless wonders i will explain when i was running the area and my stuff was not loaded and left for next way to get out of town?Strike ONE i get a hold of a god father main supervisor and tell him of the problem as his blood pressure rises pretty fast he says thanks i will take care of it and he is not bull shiiten He goes to see this rubber supervisor and has a talk calls me and tells me next trip out let me know about and i will go and watch the loading and unloading of trip !And seconds later i get a call over the radio this stuff cant go no help or time and the jerk is inside standing doing nothing as his crew is sitting reading the paper!Here comes the ending to his ass?My god father supervisor friend goes in side and sees this rubber jerk and the whole room cleared out as the yelling started And a few seconds late they are in the office with the chief end of joke The chief gave the rubber a few days off to start with .But from then on when ever anything was to leave tow and shipped out of town No more bull it was gone ? Once that was out what happen i never hard any problems moving a thing but if people were short and needed help to load up i sent it and was told over the radio thanks !And one time just before this event i go out after work before i had my sons stopped had a hamburger and one beer went home right to bed but on my Friday night out as i was eating my burger a low life supervisor stands up starts calling me name and making remarks about what i do at work!He is the same size as i am 6'4"real close to 200lbs I put down my nice warm burger and go up to this jerk and we start yelling and name calling face to face!And not much longer the hands are flying back and forth but i push this jerk into mens room and beat the snot out of his ass and he was out ?I picked him up dragged his face to the toilet and put his head in and flushed and walked out of mens room !No one said a word to me as i sat down finished eating my burger One great person i have know for a long time came over to me asked me is he still in one piece i told him look in mens room and he did the jerk was on the floor bleeding and sleeping they woke him up with lots of ice cubes and took him to hospital next day at work the jerk comes up to me and say sorry for starting the fight and walked away never talked to each other again end of the story!

As i was doing this and word was out no more problems with a thing a my work area ,but you felt good getting work done i would cook up ribs hot sauce chips what ever and bring it in for my crew of workers the idea was to make it happen and a nice clean safe place to work and the answer to this was so many people wanted to work my area no problems with this in place it has one more event Very little if any sick calls not many if any People were working happy telling joke and doing to together no fights or yelling matches it turned out to be a fun happy place to work !And if i needed any help on any thing it was done never missed a thing And when fines came out for missing the trips out of town did not see any fines with happy place to work every thing went and done ?I even was called into chiefs office and asked how is everything going because no fine we have never seen it like this?And here is another one come holidays more trucks and boxes were needed to store thing in due to weather and the fines?But for about 4yrs when did it the stuff was not needed and returned empty helped save lots of bucks from the company in there pocket and i was having fun and kept it going for years .And just as you are happy and doing it all in a happy way i get asked if you want to be supervisor i would tell them no thanks i like working and walking on my own feet with my own two hands Not a suck butt sorry !I like it like this but cant see why every time i put in transfer to different dept i would be told so much bull !just i case what ever dept, one that i really wanted and went on my free time and learned about it as well as a real good friend would teach me all kinds of information just in case !Take the test pass,talk out interview no problem 30days goes by and you get the reason why you did not get the job ready for this .once i was told i don't talk enough? cant think that out when you are glued to a computer for 8hrs ?Am i suppose to talk to the computer and wait for a answer? here is a good laugh on there part ?I was told we will give you a starting date for dept but first you are to go and walk up a few flight of stairs. Being disabled we want to make sure you are strong enough ?So you are called to meet a supervisor and a few other workers at the large building just walk along with them ?As this happens, it is Five story building So as the tie jockey starts to walk does not say a word to me but i just follow along as he starts walking the stairs right behind him all the way up a few other people did not make it they had to stop a few time to catch there breath But as i passed them on the way up all the way to the top of the building no problem still not a word to me but you can see this jerk looking at me !

As we all get to the top a few people huffing and puffin i just walked around looking at things up there as the tie jockey asks me how am i doing i tell him fine what else are we going to do next?He said nothing and walked away not a word as we all start going down again i am right behind him !I am willing to bet he thinks being a amputee i don't walk right sorry wrong answer!I try like the rest for years and then some .When we get all the way down walk around a few more steps he comes over to me asks me again what kind of disabled problem did i have i told him leg was gone due to motorcycle accident he say you would never know ?I tell thanks as we are walking he comes up to me and says they will call me soon for the job dept i wanted .Good luck and walked away as i go back to my one area and start again my friend calls me and says they never saw this happen before to any one for any reason And i was a first !Now i wonder why low life company reason for the mind games again and as always a few months go by still no job transfer after Six months i try again .And this is the icing on the cake after taking the test with bad double vision and i asked to take it after i get the new eye glasses but am told no you have to be there for that test on that day or else! And to make it worse this was on my day off to come in for the test as i did I cant even read the paper the test is on have no idea what is in writing but i try to do the best i can ?Sure enough next day i was told you failed the test both reading and math,i tried to tell them i cant even see the paper enough to read a thing as i was laughed at by the person she grabs the papers and walks away i wish i could have at least seen the test and the reading because two days later i had the glasses i needed ?Don t you wonder where the jerks are who told them to make you take the tests I would love to how they do with double vision?   It took a few days to relax enough to talk about the games being played by the company nothing like a cat and mouse game i am the mouse being chased by a smelly cat?And it is not over yet ?because a few years later i go to a different job interview and talk about games here we go again Now i go to the main building of the company and talk with some people who i have seen before in fact the person who called the 911 when i was smashed up real good is the

same person asking me questions !I felt way out of place but what the
hell see what happens next as we walk around he does not say one
word about the accident, nothing In fact this is the first time i have
seen him from the accident till now .I was never told what happen to
him or were he went or did!And now he is running this job Dept few
minutes later we are done he tells me we will be calling you soon don't
worry and let you know because we have a few more people to talk
with for this job ?I tell thanks and walk out the door out to lunch all
the way back to my work area once there i sit wondering what was
going on how does this person feel i talked with about the job because
i am still alive due to him and his actions ?I wonder if i will ever know
about this from him ?And i was letting it go and working my way
around it all and forgetting about it !Sure enough the phone rings and
it is the guy i talked with early today with? Now what is going on ?As
he starts talking i almost fall off the chair in shock !Yes you got the job
start Sunday a week away no problem do you want it let us know after
you think about it okay thanks bye AS i sit there out to lunch in shock
cant believe this ?now i have to make up my mind yes or no to do this
job Yes to get out of here and do something new for work !or no not
interested which one is it think about it for a while and have some
kind of a answer to do it with! So the rest of the day out to lunch
wondering what do i do take the job or turn it down which way to go
do i go ?Wonder more and more try to reason with the picture which
way is the best to do I want out of the current job so bad and fast to
use the brain doing something else and feel better !As i am out to lunch
it is time to go home and this will be interesting to go home even more
and wonder for a while till i have the answer,Not to jump at the first
move of any kind .   As i get almost home with the slow driving home
looks great place to think even more away from the job helps think
about the new one to come if Possible .Sons all home now from school
all waiting for me to get home i fix them something to eat and make
sure they do there home work right off the top as i was started to
wonder some more i just go into bedroom to think a little more And
try to come up with a good answer for tomorrow at work .Time to Get
dinner ready soon as i am trying to relax quick dinner burgers and rice
some veggies for sons and back into peace and quiet And way back i
have a thought for the better !Being union person you have 30days to

work if not and you don't want to stay at current job back to old one !Great i think i will take the job and if i don't work out i will go back to where i started and try again later after i come up for air and take a break from the whole picture .What a re leaf i have the answer and i will call them back and let them know about my answer on the job but i wonder how soon before i start this new one i know there is a starting date on there books when they want you there and work maybe about 7 working days any way we will see by tomorrow !Now all the pressure is off my back what a re leaf feel better already And while sons eat dinner real soon i will take a shower and try to do more relaxing to get the brain to take a rest and fade away from the stress! Just a i hop out of shower sons are home for dinner great timing walk to kitchen and start passing around dishes of food as sons sit down and start eating away !Now it is turning out to be a better day but sure is a long one! after dinner is done and sons are watching TV all is quiet i am ready for bed now and only about 730pm have a couple of hours to go it has worked better when in bed by 900 to 930 pm as leaving for work at 515 am and wake up the birds on the way in not many cars seen that early in the morning hour drive later and i am there no problem with special parking with handicap spots wide open not problem .One part about driving hour each way to work it is relaxing like doing something to get your mind off the past weather good or bad it sure does help forget about it all And just think about the nuts in front of you driving and look out for them just in case ?I have seen so many dumb move fender benders and bad accidents from the nuts in front of you !And another part going threw this battle zone devoice is another mess. Nothing simple maybe breathing and that is about it After being sent to strange doctors to talk to because you had a head trauma is just as bad !Asking you questions makes you wonder where he came from I try to tell them of a person who put hands and feet threw walls yelling at you to do want they tell you or even if a son gets hurt by one partner that is not important noes not matter but if look or say something wrong you are put threw the cleaners and dry cleaned one two three .One part i had a Doctor try to come to court and talk when the other side found out about the doctor they were set up at another court room and building wondering where is was as not being told about the sudden switch room being pulled !Another thing is when you tell the judge who has turned into a rotten nut running loose and you say who and are told that is not what the court was told !When fighting for kids be ready for the most rotten and event you ever say because that is what happens When you have cops come to court on your side due to the fun and game plated on you when other side see the cops things get turned around and settled before you get to say a word and done ! And it is very hard to do when your kids want to be with one parent and try to say that in court watch out i had sons say where they wanted to be one way or another but took years of trying just to do that some judges you can talk with other before you say your name you are labeled bad guy and you did not say a thing try talking to a judge after that little event But once it happens you are okay just letting the judge be leave in you watch out. Even after i had the kids and the judge asks if some one else wants to see kids and says no what a ,thumper ! Once it is over with keep eye on kids i had one kid real made and one real quiet and both wondering as i took kids to doctor to talk to To make sure they will be okay if any thing else is needed to help them threw this !Because i went threw the same thing after it was over with and i was with one parent i was one Mad kid for years on end,no one went near me or said a thing to me because fights were always happen no matter who or what just need a reason why and it would happen !Fights in school were real bad being 6'2"about 175 lbs to big always the last one no matter what you do you are at the end of the line .That get old and fights get going .Once in high school i was the smallest i was 6'4"I was with guys 6'5" one guy was 6'7" but it was good because no one was dumb enough to mess with you or your friends peace and quiet again .With the past event i am making sure my sons don't go down that road no need for it now at all!Even after some time has come and gone no problem still little made about the whole thing and one part i did not start it But i put a finish to it and helped three kids in the long run!After that i am half way threw the mess court with kids in done and the part with work is being dragged on and i will hang in there i will bet the games are just starting to be played out. Because once and a while i will talk with people about what was told and what was going around with any truth to it ,And i don't feel like getting up set for a while but it make you wonder a little more as always Because learning FBI will not even talk with you is bad enough as to you getting any where with them asking for help and nothing you have been to congressman and nothing no help again you call and write govt people like us dept of justice you might as well scream because no help from them. And to say the least ,but the city cops are worthless or i don't speak enough English it does not matter nothing !One part very interesting is the insurance people what they paid out due to someone signing your name is unreal right after they tell you ya we paid the insurance policy and that it but wont tell you about how much but you read the papers on it and see the amount another unreal one hits again !   After trying to draw up a list to see where you have or have not been is real long .When you have been to so many you better draw up a list just to make sure you do not do a replay on the same one !One part that i will like to say about is while all the places and people you write and it takes months and years just for answers and ideas to do more but i have one i hope you don't pop off your chair because one place i wrote to is the leader of it all and yes i did write to them president of us states of America Ready to hear the answer ?So this person at the white house and says sorry we cant help we were told differently about this are you sure about it ? And you send then copies of Doctors writing reported as well as police writing and nothing for answer you try to call them after being put on hold for a good time frame and i mean minutes and lots like the first 20min and i tried to call again this time 25min nothing on hold again!And i gave up But the letter is good enough as always sorry we cant do a thing on the matter!Have you ever wondered how mess up it really is what i am baffled about in America when you hear about catching a bad guy who did Murder or Bank Robbery and in jail and you hear about other for 25yrs and either gave up or where caught !I wonder how long before some one Gets off there chair warmer and does a thing about this one !I have come to think A bolt of lighting is better off and burn the low life and this way save money going to jail most likely will lie thee way out of it, So mother nature burns the bugger!   Just so you have a better picture this is the second president i wrote the First one said and in writing we will look in to this and get in touch with you as soon as possible It was a shame because another president was in office and i never heard from the First one i wrote to .Now after all of these thought how messed up it really is. I Think about so many of these as i drive in to work .After about 45 minutes and getting closer to work i wipe it all out get to work and feel re leaved and in a good state of mind ready to work best possibly can! and today in the path of on the way to work is the day i make the call and tell them i will take the job and when do i start it?Wondering how long before it happens?And just to make sure it is not stopped by any one from happening!once at work my locker is cleaned out and nothing there just in case all my uniforms are all placed in a pile ready to be trashed or filed ?And not a word to a soul about any thing or any time !Just be gone once and for all i hope ? I get back to my work area sit down relax wait and see what happens next?As the clock get to 0800am i call this person and tell him glad to take the job but when do i start to have all the fun ?And today is Monday to start with maybe Sunday i hope but next i am told one week on Sunday morning not this Sunday but next !Great i tell him thanks see ya soon .Good bye?As my head puffs up happy as hell i just walk around smiling feel pretty lucky after all this going threw and on trying to get to different dept at last has happen .maybe being in a different place to work the dreams and thought of getting run over will drop out and not bother me after all of this .I really hope so it would help a lot. I was told about the new job doing what i have already been doing answer the phone and list the information in the computer in a matter of seconds while they are on the phone is no big deal glad to do it .something close to what i have done already will help as to have a pay raise will help a lot only a few bucks in my pocket more, But more to help with sons and the house we have! All i do now is hope for the best ? All of this is the course of working and trying to do better I have seen so many people give up on half of what i have been threw and i still cant see why give up!As i have tried to say i lived a hit so bad to my body that could have killed two other people already and i still want to work and get on with life getting better i hope soon .I have learned mind over matter i have named it for example when a doctor tell you it will take six months before you walk after loosing leg and Three months later i am going back to work and once there being told where have you been on vacation and cant even see i lost a leg all of that really helps get threw it mind over matter Because it hurt trying to walk but all i thought about is working and before long get up pop on leg walk away i used to walk every morning up and down the streets to build up the strength to walk there were bloody sores on leg but i blanked it out and kept walking till it was just to sore to pick up the leg walk get home pop off leg clean up the wound and next day try some more and it worked because like i said three months after loosing leg i was back to work .And after this other mess i was in trying to kill me at work i just blanked it out and got better with talking and walking and a little bit longer i was at work again and working away not thinking of what happen and i did it But the problem is company making my life rotten to get me out and no more information on what really happen to me .And the good part after feeling better working and getting some where with the beat up body was Great to do With that so many people would tell me what happen who were there when i was hit and put down .Only the dieing tie jockey company will say different .And to make sure about this piece by piece i called wrote and talked to many people only to be told not a accident How about when you talk to doctors who do this every day putting human beings back together daily !Why would say and write injury not accident related!Because i have said it i did not walk into moving tractor! I wonder how many people could make it threw this by there selfs,I did AS i write to explain about this there is plenty more about the games from many people and companies all working together As you get the run around with the word Head injury Like your brain hoped out and your skull is on empty. The funny part there are plenty of people out thee who have not had any type of injury and could not have made it half way threw where i have been already and did it threw and made it when i said i was treated like i have a part missing but i still made it back to work I hope this helps people get threw what ever they are doing and remember not to give up or give in !I learned to just smile and keep on going that made them watching me mad as hell because could not bother me not this time or the next !And this came from the one Doctor H who made sure i make it because he knew i wanted to get to work there are a few more events i will say about just to see just a few on what was done to me at work and it went on and on .And to start with easy games being played every call if it went threw was heard by supervisor who would just look like nothing was going on every call for what as i said in past would not even let sons threw after 7 times trying .And at first they would just smile at out you and tell you have a good day!After they found out about EEOC and the charges filed it turned in to whats wrong cant you hear me you better check you hearing Or the best one to show how low they are Whats wrong with you after the head trauma . something wrong cant you think or remember and smile at you and walk away. This happen more and more but to Make you feel even better and it was like a tail following you around every where you go walk to mens room and the tail was out side the door waiting ,If i walked to lunch room and picked up a cup of Tea they would be right next to you looking at your cup. But the last one was so close to loosing there teeth ,I thought about it,I sat down in lunch room by my self eating lunch and they sat on other side of the same table making remarks about what i was eating so some how i took out the remote control for the hearing aid and shut it off .now peace and quiet as they saying something i have no idea about what but a few seconds later they got up and walked away. But it seemed every time i took a little walk i was followed ? And it gets to be so much fun at this new job i decide time to go back and i have only been there two weeks i had enough of this And the same person i talked with to get the job i talked to telling him i want to go back to old job?had enough of the games as i said that he looked at me like sure,And he says i will check on it and get back to you tomorrow okay!I go back sit down cleaned out my desk threw most of the papers right in trash can and a few other people watching me. And i go and try to sign on my computer and it is all locked up no matter what i touch nothing happens no response to a thing. So now i call the computer repair techs and about 3 minutes later they come in and said someone did this to your unit with your sign on I lost it got slammed the door and walked down the hall like a steaming train engine !I was all the way across the building in seconds look behind me sure enough the supervisor was not far behind me .Whats up what is wrong i tell him about the computer tech told me about someone getting into my unit!Now he gets red in the face and tells me he will take care of it don't worry it wont happen again!Lets walk back and see what i can do about this !We walk back i sit down he make a few calls and more people come down and right to my computer they found out what time on what day and who it was that did this sneaking on my unit All i was told to do was change the pass word and don't worry it will not happen again!and they would not tell me who it was and i wonder who the sneak was but who cares they will deal with it !as i changed my pass word i was able to sign in and start my day of fun at work !And as always no one asked one a thing about it from other workers And after so many little event like this i went to a company person to talk with And was told they work with disabled workers and the company to work things out .It was not much time before i learned what a waste of time and effort!No matter what i told them about the problems i would be better off learning how to fly Nothing was done about anything i told them what the problems taken place And to see what a scum sucking low life person They to were called by EEOC and it was about the charges and were told to make a statement !And what came out of there mouth was taken out of EEOC statement and it had to do with the color of my skin being a disabled person. I was hoping EEOC would hit this jerk with charges but what happened they did not talk with me any more about a thing .Same person who said i should go to church more and pray to get thing done now i learned why. They were full of hot air And this all came to me by a lawyer telling me what was done and took place in the deposition what a joke !That really bothered me for some time it went right along with the lies from the company only this jerk made a real bad remark .And i see how the company covers this up that person was no longer around at that job and was doing something else real fast .The picture where they talked to all the VP at work and fill them in was stopped. I tried to talk with a CEO at work after this had happened !And i cant see how they were made CEO !You could not put all there brains on the head a pin there is not enough to cover it !I am not kidding around. They have so many people under them helping them all they do is sit and read the news paper not much else. They only work short days at work i have never seen them past 8hrs no matter what happens,They don't write a thing have either a recorder or own sectary ,They don't drive, Have some one drive them around where ever the want to go!And what i don't gets, Even there family is in another state either close or far away and for years they go back and forth to home and back on the weekend,So how do they get the CEO job After seeing all of this he says can i help you sit down and lets talk,Another waste of time again they could care less what you say Any way i tried talk about the cover up and the phone calls we will kill you and the low life supervisors following me around And i was told I will check around and get back with you soon!I might as well go buy lottery tickets i have a better chance of wining before the CEO does a thing about any thing taken place .And nothing like smashing your own face into the brick wall waiting for help?Sure i just walk back to my area again fell really down after all of the bull. And as i get the computer going and get ready to do something ?I work area supervisor calls me over to his desk and says lets go out in the hall and have a talk !And sure off we both walk threw the door and i am standing up against the wall he starts with the bull. Sorry but you cant go back to your old work area not any more ,Being a disabled person it is not good for you and you have to stay here for a while?I tried to talk and tell him the union rules about work ares and the other way to do thing And told no not being disabled and after you did the charges of not accommodated you!you can check but you will be here Dot the part is you have done a great job here people call asking for you because you do it in a hurry and just as it is in the books to do So you are better off just staying here and forget about going back ?I don't say a word and walk away pissed as hell .I will call union EEOC and who ever i need to this is bull again I sit and call a supervisor friend and he tells the same thing they will not let you back due to disability!Bull see ya i hang up and go over to supervisor listen i don't feel to good i want to go home and he says see ya take care see you later !I just get into van and go home to hell with them all! . How are you suppose to keep it up and hang in there this is the pits i know so many people who did just what i am trying to do and no problem done and back to old work area no questions asked And after calling EEOC and leave a message for them to call me back i sit and wait !called union people told them the same thing sit and wait for they call ?After waiting most of the day still not one call back to me .I am getting tired of all of this bull being pushed and pulled at the same time over and over!And i wonder again even more why is this taken place !All i wanted to do is work and be okay !Now i wonder if that is a good choice!And here it is almost 5pm and not one call the day will be over soon and nothing!I get out the papers i have from the company there is a person to call about this and problems at work again so i call and talked to this person after a few minutes i will see this person tomorrow and talk together about this i hope it helps do something soon !After that i feel like my whole day was waste of time ?right down the s hitter and real quiet the rest of the day glad when it is over to get to bed and get some sleep i hope And i was tossing and turning a good part of the night and walking back and forth on crutches cant sleep much more and i an up here it is 330am in the morning and i cant sleep So i get a cup of tea sit up peace and quiet sit and think wonder what will happen we will see i want to get back to old place to work !and nothing but trouble !After drinking the cup of tea i go and get dressed cant sleep might as well i sit back now at the counter and wonder on and on what to do about this and in about and hour i have to get to work and see some more of the games i wonder it is to early to call any one about this bull So worry about it later .I get in check on sons walk back and looking at clock soon i will drive to work and i hope i make it i am very much out to lunch with thoughts !Try to eat something before i go some toast and another cup of tea. Short while later i am out the door driving to work and on the far right side of the road taking my time driving in. I am suppose to see this new person at 0900am and have a talk even bought the paper from the accident for him to try and read .I hope he does do and sees for him self what happen.   Once at work i am very slow walking like so what is next and the guards are up once at my desk sitting down seeing more people around me is the same old some old thing not a word .get my computer going and sit and wait and see whats next this is 0700 to start with now and by 0830am not a call !man it is a long morning to start with already and at 0845 i leave walk up to the room to meet this person to talk with have all my papers in a thick folder and once there sit in a large room by self and wait .And at 0900am this tall person with a ugly tie on walks in asks my name we shake hands he has a seat i start to tell him about things and how they are going ?After about 20 minutes of non stop talking i stop and wait to see what he says about it all?Inf you ever have that feeling it is not to good here and this person i am talking to ?And right off the top he tells me that is not what he was told or what he thinks has happened, strike one ! So now i put out the paper work from the doctors who put my skull and body back together and show this person .As i can feel the blood pressure going up just the way this person talks about and saying that is not how it happen i tried to keep my cool and tel him it is truth to this event and the seven holes in my skull were ice pick or board with nails in it ?No i don't think so listen what hospital were you in i will go and read more about this ,But did not look at me as he said this?something is not right here ?So i give him the name of hospital and the talk ended very fast right there he walked out and i walked back to the work spot very upset to this low life i was just talking with !And from then on had a feeling something is very much wrong here !What where or what is it maybe when has to do with it .I am off tomorrow we will see ?And i just happen to go to hospital and walk up to records dept on the floor and as i said Hi to a person i have seen so many times,And i ask her for my file and the paper work she walks away and short while later comes tells me the file is not there ?Walks away as tells me there is another place to look for it comes back and tells me again No it is gone i asked any way of seeing who looked at it last ?Leans over and says a person the company insurance dept were last to see it ?I tell thanks and walk away!Now i know the dieing company was the one again who did it ! And i was driving home Mad as a Dog, There is something very well messed up here !All the way home all i can think of is the low life i talked with already i beat who had it done Once home i called some people i know who work the company and told them of this person i talked with and was told he is a real low life had his ass kicked years ago at another city for snooping around and making remarks about people working, They kick the snot out of him!Now i know why he talks like a real jerk and it shows!It is not even lunch time and i am home good time to lay down and take a nap after having so much fun and games. I head for the bed room and down and out for a while !Almost 2hrs later i am up just before sons get home from school do the snacks for them and ready for them to eat when they get in!I have nothing else planned for my days off maybe just take it easy and do nothing .i walk back to bed room have a seat lay back and the phone rings .Union rep telling sorry we cant help maybe next time !Still up set as always worthless union rep .Do nothing as always Two days off go by pretty fast and tomorrow i go back to see the rest of it ?And as i get going to work again driving in to work i wonder what will go down this day?AS i pull in park the van walk in sit down and get started i see the people at work all talking to each other ?But not a word to me on anything or about any thing now almost 1100am one one by one the other workers are walking out

of here but where are they going for what ever,And a supervisor tells
me to cover the place till they all get back?and walks away before i can
ask him what going on?It only lasted about 45minutes to a hour and
no information on what was going on to me ?As they are all back and
getting thing going i was called to go to lunch room and talk with
supervisor ? So off i go walking to lunch room once there i see the
supervisor and sit at a table and wait to see the fun. Was told i do good
what i am doing people were here talking about there work and how
they are doing as well!After about 3 or 4 minutes i was told by supervisor
to go back to my work spot and have a nice day! This is a pile of bull
and something is not right here but i will never know about the very
quiet information because the same person i just talked with i the same
person who told the workers not to talk to me because of the EEOC
charges !And i know there is more to this because a few days later she is
gone not in are work area any more don't even know if she is still
working for the company But was told something was changed at work
because of EEOC and the current charges pending That is how i have
seen the company cover them up so many times in so many ways it is
the same thing all to be gone ! Almost every person i talk with is no
longer there Even so time ago there was a great supervisor he did a
great job and work with people real good you do your job and he does
his no problem. He was around and knew about my accident and what
was missing i even asked him about it and was told yes your are right
that did happen !But when a job opening came for supervisors he was
next to get it but because he was very straight person instead they made
him take early retirement or get fired which is real rotten again by
company so he retired asap! Super nice person gone !And some real
butt kisser got the job any way. I really hope by writing about a few
events to help people so they don't have to go threw the same mess .
And in the long run of this picture it has not gotten any better from
the start till now same thing. Only part i really like when talking to
Doctor H and he has thought me many thing i still carry with me deep
inside thanks to his great words. Because he taught me so many ways
to keep cool and not snap because it is not my fault and all the games
from supervisors playing on me all i did was blow it off other wise they
would have a few free lumps on the heads for free !And this was even
in court with plenty of dieing lawyers trying to make my life as rotten

as possible be instead i wrote it all down dated it sent it in and lawyers were busted pretty good .And no more run around from them!and there are a few who get away with to much bull and they work for the us afterward a waste of flesh and no brains at all and we pay there wages!Once at the Doctors office it turns out to be a very safe place to talk And not to keep looking around to see who is coming or going . Because of that the pain goes down a lot and it feel real Good inside And i believe he thought me how to get my sons to a safe place they are pretty happy for a long time. There is a small part to write about there is plenty of times the games were played And seemed non stop for years and day after day !As you cant relax more and more and your days off get changed weekly instead of yearly that you bid for Your body starts to really slid down the tubes .It turns out you go two or three days with no sleep and very little eating And try to drive to work like that is very hard and dangerous and thats to keep in touch with a real Doctor H is why i am still around and not 6 feet down and it came close to it! But one day at work trying to relax and do my job I go and talk with a two sided union he does company favors and union favors So i tell him it is a good thing no one comes in here with a gun and start blasting away Because at the time on the news there were a few that had taken place .A lot of people were nervous and watching around just in case But after saying that i was given time off from work pending a hearing to loose my job and even worse was company supervisor making all kinds of remarks to you as well as the phone calls were listened to as well and the old saying the pressure is on! has taken being watched like a hawk any where or any thing i did And a short time later the stress has gotten me .I was shaking so bad bit my tung so many times trying to talk about it and when you go for help at a union rep tells you sorry i heard about it you did not even tell him yet?But you will be fired What the hell is going on now .But instead of loosing it i called the Doctor and asked for help?Was told go home i will call them you take of your self get home ans watch out !I go back in side having a hard time walking nervous as hell tell supervisor my doctor will call them i am going home as i am walking away i hope i make it to my van as the shaking is so bad i could not put the key into door lock to get into my own van!Due to shaking .And now is not to good of a time to drive a van!I. just sat there for a while and i don't mean 5 minutes and drive away I put the seat back closed my eye and tried to relax enough to get the shaking to stop as well as the bad double vision!Real close to 40 minutes later i start to slow down breathing is getting better,eye sight is getting there as the shaking is slowing down !This is a cold day out as well so start up the van and sit there a while long as i am getting warm and feeling better so now i try to drive home As i drive slow as always and taking my time as t get further and further away from here i feel better i get right home it is early afternoon and i am home way before sons get here so i try to lay there and relax as much as possible don't feel like eating a thing,but a nice warm cup of tea will help ! Drinking a cup of tea nice and warm is great trying to relax the phone rings Doctor H calls to make sure i am okay and to come to his office tomorrow early in the day Great much needed to talk about the games and the puppets And now i wonder what will happen back to work some time later or what else to do?I will find out tomorrow after talking to doctor H And And i am suppose to sleep tonight, fat chance to much on the brain. And wonder what will happen about work 27yrs down the tubes as always!but time will tell me one way or another !Like work or no work !really feel rotten about all the fun and games God for bid if i tell the truth !Something strange i have seen like so much and many lies going on what happens when truth comes along?What i have seen and been put threw is the answer Cant handle the truth and labeled the Bad Guy !You told them what happen and not made up with the facts well as in writing !All my life i believe just tell the truth no problems. Here is proof to this How does a semi of apple 2 computers turn up missing and the proof about what happen when at supervisor home a truck of apple 2s is in front ?When one flying low life scared have my just his butt beat down the street stays away from you so badly could walk down the rows at work and boxes are missing and more than one and this would happen a few days a weeks but the company does not even write up this event as well ?Just pays the missing stuff out of there pocket and no paper work to prove it as well! Nice trick !and has been going on for years on end!The other parts is the low life with sticky fingers don't even talk or tell you a thing !But not had to see what taken place and now you can see way so many camera"s on watch our off ?Only one with the keys is in it as well? Same when i was put down tape is missing only one with key to lock up is lieing supervisor ?Another nice trick again ! All of this kept under the rug cant do show and tell to good all the tie jockeys doing the lieing when you talk to them they retired asap not a word i saw this so many times person after person on the upper level still a low life!Never mind son had dinner watching TV maybe bed for them soon we will see and maybe i can try and see what happens next . Doctor H tomorrow will fill me in with some ways and ideas we will see what happens .Either i get put on certain level for discipline ?Due to this first time ever in 27yrs of service Of i am fired and gone in the morning?How the hell do i sleep with all of the thoughts going on now?Long night coming up soon!After dinner was the best part soon sons will be in bed and night over .Have to be at Doctors at 1000am tomorrow and see it all get better or worse ?I clean up after sons are done eating tell them i am in my bed room if you need anything just let me know about it homework done everything else can wait .As the night gets here and sons hit the bed i turn in and flip and flop with thoughts trying to wonder what to do next and it is eating me up ! not sleeping so might as well grab a book and try to read and maybe sleep will win and i get to together after all .Not much thinking about the book i toss it and just lay in bed to with all about all of the fun i have had for years of work till i was run over never did or have anything wrong at work till this cover up and the Games with it!And not much longer i will be at Doctors office and get this off my mind for good ?And by 0800 i get in van and head for doctors office and a few times i was there before the doctor was at his office thinking about this as i drive maybe this morning we will see .And i have been driving and trying to keep my mind on what i have been doing and this morning is one very strange one with the idea i may be working or may be not ?Sure enough i beat the doctor to his office and there i a bench type seating in the hall way to his office so have a seat and wait !Next ed time elevator comes up and the doors open up and the Doctor walks off and say a Good morning and we both walk to his office As he unlocks the door we step in i peel off the jacket and sit down wait for the Doctor tell me when ,and i walk into his special place for talking is Great very quiet room with lots of windows to see the whole town we are in And very relaxing place to sit and talk As he closes the door we start and i am told why it is this way And i am done working due to the mind games from the company with the lies at 48yrs old and done is not sitting to good but it will not stop is i keep working and they want to fire you, you are wasting your time at work and the pay back of bothering you will not stop ? After a short while And here it comes and i am told You Are Done Working Stay home for a while either find another job or do something else they are not going to stop bothering you and you don't need it after all you have been threw!Due to the games this is what is going on we cant talk or write to them it means nothing .So this is it you stay home for a while till the pain goes down as well as not sleeping comes back in time Stay home on medical for three years right to the limit of Three years and either go back or the end!And i have agreed because he is right. It will take some time but i can do something else and i will. i did not tell a soul about this move to stay home But first i have to get a few thing s taken care of like insurance Social security .And what ever else possible to make sure sons and i are okay Right on the way home from Doctor H I went to social security and filled out the papers to get started !And just as i was told it will not stop as well because in social security when you talk with a person with a very hi IQ of maybe 2 or 3 because things started right there with a person who is better off standing on the corner of the street and selling pencils, Because trying to tell them what medical trauma you went threw as well as the problems still there and being told you look fine are you sure that happen ?And to make it very much a bad move on me because every time i filled it out all the papers never were seen and was told am i sure about it and i did not loose them .No there the puppet heads who lost the papers three times and if you think that is okay how about no income to live on to start with and the other part even worse it took almost 9 months to go threw there system and that was not enough But 30 days later a judge had to make the answer if i was disabled or not ?And i wrote the judge a thank you because he was nice enough to know about amputee as well as the rest of the medical problems !Till this day i have stayed away from social security in my town because of that and i tried to move during the summer to a place very warm most of the year and i get a letter from SS telling me to be looked at if i was still disabled .So way in another state i go and was told by them what is wrong With the person who sent this paper work about being disabled now and always will be i told this person thank you because he called the muffin head where it was started and filled them in because ever since it has been fine and no problems . And if that is not enough go for start help is even worse the people there have no IQ I will beat you they are plugged in every morning all recorded and charged The reason i say that is the person on my case to help with the food and funds says i have to much income and as i tried to show her tell her it did not matter because turned down twice And to be in a place and nothing in the English words is playing tape after tape in some other Language and seeing other people there asking what is that tape about to other people and the people at the desk make sure there glass was closed and did not have to hear it as well!No matter how i tried telling the thing i was out of work sons don't work still in school and was turned down i still would like to see this person in the streets just to flip them off with a few hand moves !After all of this what do i do and how after being told just wait and see it will be okay is like holding your breath for days and see what happens after a short when you hit the floor hope there is someone to pick you up !After some of this i will share with you another fun day at home I believe you need a good laugh will it is time!This is a nice December evening only about 730pm all the sons are watching TV and movies very quiet only about 25 degrees out side had a big dog was named Bear some type Shepard and rototiller biggest dog I have seen in years from a lady who was tired of taken care of him because she worked two or three jobs with two kids around 12 or 13 yrs old she was very busy maybe enough to sleep very little gives me this very friendly dog when i had him standing up with his feet on my shoulder and at 6'3" 200lbs was very easy for this great dog he did not fit on a single bed his legs were to long !But any way in the day time i had the dogs in a large fenced in place for the dogs size was about 10 foot by 30 or 40 feet they had a large dog house with heater and 5gal water bucket This day was freezing rain so the dog was in the house walking around i think it was time for a walk before it is much later I put on the 10foot leash and out the front door we go walking bear goes right to the grass covered with ice to do his thing and it is freezing up pretty soon afterwards Bear turns real fast pulls me the other way in seconds as my feet both go out from under me as i try to keep standing but one leg goes one way snaps the other leg with the lightweight fiberglass goes one way and snaps as i was falling over with two legs breaking i put out one arm to break the fall it snaps the hand has the leash it was full length straight out hits the ground and snaps now both legs and both arms busted ,Bear starts barking as i start whistling and people come out like my two sons and the lady next door who gave me Bear see me laying there i start telling them to call for ambulance about 15minutes late as they pull and try to put me on a board in to ambulance and then stretcher i start yell hurting was pretty good i lated there till the ER once they say more like this put me out woke up two days later with casts on both arms and one leg with a cast and one half leg all wrapped up in bandages with splits around it as well what a mess and feel like crap to start with and if that is not bad here is the punch line no insurance coverage. I did not know but the coverage from work was stopped as i wait for and was told Medicare i was covered but was not Now what do i do the great hospital sends me a letter a few weeks later when i was home telling me it was on the hospital because i have no coverage And after reading that letter one son held up for me to read helped because one week after being in hospital and sent home helped being bed ridden for TWO months what a mess again!It comes out to be the end of February when the casts were off and tried to walk and move and after two months with fake leg on it took another month to get the leg to fit the man made one as i squeezed into he old one and only about hour a day before i could take much more !I try to laugh and say just in time for spring thaw before i can go out and walk !And the other side of this was my sons saw me like this busted up helped a lot feeding me and washing me up helped a lot thank god they were okay as well After that was very careful i walk out side and in bad weather I cant go out and walking! This all happen as i just was pulled from work a few weeks later And after working is no more i called EEOC with the dragged on charges still pending due to the lieing company and there Hench men pondering around T told them i was done with work due to the games being played no problem .They to were wondering When it was going to be settled as well,I told them who knows But is there any way of filing more charges?No but we will let you know when possible to do so ?Because after the depositions and all the input from doctors lawyers all was to be done but some how it was dragged on lost what ever the crew of puppets can do is being done to never settle it ?And years go by and i mean more than Ten still waiting for anything and nothing shows but what was pulled is so far out i cant see as well as other how this is done and nothing happens ,After seeing this i had a few thoughts related to this Because after this why put to jail people who Rob banks ,Deal drugs,what ever because when you get a paper and it says wages and you are out of work five years earlier and you write IRS and go there just for a answer but get nothing but the company tell your lawyer it is wages and it is not but it was suppose to be your bit of funds from EEOC charges as you read the letter saying there was never charges as well from EEOC Or your lawyer says it was worth$75,000 and you get nothing try tell them what has happen means nothing and just as the lid pops off your head the amount you get is $3,500 and that was from the wages they claim you were paid And to get another laugh at you being on social security you were hit again with high taxes claim as wages !Have you ever wondered how much horse shit they smoked and were in some space suite flying around because what that was in writing and that the low life company wrote are no where near what happen to you .And no body will do a damn thing about no matter how you try !Better of pissing out the window It might be worth more than what you received ! Now after you have had enough and tried to tell so many people and it means nothing Maybe you can tell me how some scum of the earth can do this and not go to jail or fined for all the lies and games ?And at the begin g when i said the other govt dept called ADA is next to you pissing out the window and it means nothing as well And if you remember hearing the part where come to America, be free live life in a great city or country Well now you see why some many people are rich hear a vast amount and some have or are being caught for the lies and bull but there is not many laws on the books to get the real bad lieing companies they do as they please and pay who else they want with them. Ass the laws put on file to help the disabled people just was started not many years ago And the way i see it companies with no brains or guts only mess with the disabled because people not to beat up and hurt will come in and burn there butts fast So now you see how they mess with people Like a young boy gr owning up who starts all kids of things like stealing lieing what thinking they will not get caught But when they do get caught and try saying they did not do it or some one else did it That is when they get a good beating and understand to tell the truth That is a better way to live the rest of your life with truth And not have to keep looking over your shoulder the rest of your life wondering if they will catch you or go to jail!In this day and age why do some many companies go down the tubes and then they find out the owner or the one who started the company took all the funds either spent it or took off with the funds and put it some where else and look like they broke ? Now even being home and out of work it has not stopped yet the words head injury i am still getting the run around. I have tried to tell people what has happen and told ,no that could not have been it i have tried bringing in the Doctors reports and find out they will not read it or cant? One part to this is i have learned how very slow most people are when you tell them your part it is not a lie it has happen and yes i am still alive and kicking. No matter how hard i have tried it would be nice if some or half the people you talk with to understand ,It is not a lie because still have dreams of it going on but i have been tough t as well as learned how to use the thought some where else ,It took years to get it threw the cement head it was not your fault and it was done to you !I wished i had the reason but i have put a great big piece of it and have see the truth to know about it and that was part of the answer to this ,So i have tried to turn it around think the better way do and learn more things to do and try and i don't mean a little bit but try to push it out and do thing better and more interesting like i took glass classes,computer work,reading and do more have you ever wondered how much fun and a great thing that really wants to be with you could be a dog i did now have two one happy rottweiler and one happy funny boxer we go to so many place together i have gone west and back with them great company driving 1,200 to 1,400 miles and a hotel with twin double beds one bed for the dogs one for me it was funny as in the morning when people drinking there coffee not quiet awake tell you when you walk by them with both dogs you can see there eye open up real fast and step back as we get into truck and drive off better yet go to a burger place in the morning order things and pass some back to the dogs you will see people watching you real close! and no problems nothing but fun. and i have come to the very part where and i hope it helps one person and that would be the happy to a good way of life !I have seen where there is no help i have been in place where a person had a real bad accident was more busted up then me .Super smart person had a big house a big business and making money in the millions per year first his mom and dad said good by we don't know you he was married with two kids first his wife hit him with devoice papers wanting the house and some money which he could make back very easy and that was it nothing and what i saw hurt him more no one would talk to him from home and it really hurt him !I kept telling him hang in their you will be out soon to do as you please go to work and feel great but instead he took the ties from his clothes and hung him self in the bath room and was caught but not in time when they got him to hospital it was to late . Next we here his wife telling us how happy she was to have the house and money with out court ?nothing about how special this person was that she was married to for years?Not a word .I thought never to give up never,if the doctor says it will be months before you walk six weeks later i am going up and down the streets walking no problem .I was told by doctors you will be staying home because of the injurious it will take if possible years before you are working ?Well suck a egg ,Three years after this event i had my driving lic.back one and half years later after driving i was back to work cleared to work All because no i will do it one way or another ?you have to push your self by your self you feel the pain you know the part where to think or read or do things but you push your self and you will make it ,no one else really knows how you are doing but you and same as feeling people have no idea how you feel they can try but your body under you take care of it and it works .This is not over and never may be over i will talk about more when the time is right to ,Now i hope people see how special people are treated and it is not worth a nickel what is done to them just because of being disabled it is bull some day i wish i had a lawyer with a back bone but that is hard to find so for now i learned to keep it in writing it is proof and no second thoughts and not lies because i still remember it like it was done last night This is where the peace i learned to do and relax with the thoughts and bad dreams waking up screaming .It has taken some time but it did happen and i did not walk into a moving tractor but like i have said just to tell the truth and i am not a bad guy? I did nothing wrong but work and nothing to do but work and build a happy family with three great sons I love dearly and always

will thank god because no one else could help the most when needed
And just in case you wonder it is in writing all the run around taken
place and you can read it and fall over what low life do for fun is unreal
with what they get away with !

THE END